TWAYNE'S WORLD LEADERS SERIES

A Survey of the World's Literature

Sylvia E. Bowman, Indiana University
GENERAL EDITOR

JAPAN

Roy B. Teele, University of Texas

EDITOR

Mori Ōgai

TWAS 355

Mori Ōgai

Mori Ōgai

By J. THOMAS RIMER

Washington University

TWAYNE PUBLISHERS
A DIVISION OF G. K. HALL & CO., BOSTON

Library of Congress Cataloging in Publication Data

Rimer, J Thomas.
Mori Ōgai.

(Twayne's world authors series; TWAS 355: Japan)
Bibliography: pp. 127–31.
Includes index.
1. Mori, Ōgai, 1862–1922—Criticism and interpretation.
PL8II.07Z83   895.6'3'4   74–28163
ISBN 0–8057–2636–5

MANUFACTURED IN THE UNITED STATES OF AMERICA

FOR JOHN

*   *   *

How may one come to know oneself? Never by contemplation, but only by action. Seek to do your duty, and you will know how it is with you. And what is your duty? The demands of the day.

Mori Ōgai's favorite quotation
from Goethe

Contents

About the Author

Preface

An Explanatory Note

Chronology

About the Author

J. Thomas Rimer, presently Chairman of the Department of Chinese and Japanese at Washington University in St. Louis, Missouri, received his B.A. from Princeton University and his Ph.D. from Columbia University. Prior to his graduate work, he lived in Japan for seven years and was the Director of the Kobe American Cultural Center.

Mr. Rimer has also published translations of Mori Ōgai stories. His additional interests include Japanese drama. He has published a *nō* translation and a book on the modern Japanese theatre, *Toward a Modern Japanese Theatre: Kishida Kunio* (Princeton University Press, 1974). In the field of Japanese poetry, he has published translations of the modern poet Nishiwaki Junzaburō, and, with Robert Morrell, compiled a guide to Japanese poetry in the Asian Literature Bibliography Series published by G. K. Hall & Co., Boston (1975).

Preface

An introductory book on Mori Ōgai seems impossible to write. Ōgai (1862–1922) was a major force in the intellectual and cultural life of Japan's Meiji period 1868–1912), when that country was first opened to the West after more than two centuries of seclusion. His career was divided between his work in medicine, for the Japanese army, and his own artistic and intellectual pursuits. Ōgai's early years spent in Europe gave him a greater grasp of European culture than any other person in his generation, and his subsequent efforts as a translator and explicator of Western ideas, especially in the field of aesthetics, were of tremendous importance. His studies in philosophy, especially in his grasp of the relation between politics, authority, and the individual, also merit serious consideration. Ōgai felt fully the tensions between a commitment to service as a bureaucrat and the necessity for intellectual and spiritual freedom so important to a man of his character and temperament, and this source of difficulty in his own life has also made him a figure of compelling interest to students of Japanese intellectual history. Ōgai's important contributions to medical research have earned him a distinguished place in the development of science in his country.

The term "Renaissance man" does not seem an exaggeration when applied to Mori Ōgai, nor, in fact the term "Renaissance" to the period in which he lived when Japan went through so many profound changes as a culture. The very multitude of Ōgai's accomplishments may suggest that an examination only of his work as a writer will somehow prevent the reader's appreciating the full scope of his personality. Undoubtedly this is so; yet his creative works do give us the pattern of his thought and help convey a sense of the whole man.

Ōgai wrote a great deal, and in a variety of literary genres. The study that follows presumes to discuss only the more representative works with the hope of suggesting the rich pattern of ideas that lies behind even the smallest of his literary efforts. A certain amount of Ōgai's work has appeared in translation, but many representative works are not yet available in English. The danger in studying any one work is that the reader, unable to relate it to the whole corpus of Ōgai's writing, may fail to realize its significance and, understandably, may misinterpret its meaning. If this short book can introduce his major works and suggest the larger trends in Ōgai's thought, it will have succeeded to the utmost of this writer's hopes. My own study of Ōgai has convinced me (and many generations of Japanese would agree) that Ōgai is not only a commanding figure in his own tradition but a paradigm of modern man in his relentless attempt to look at the emptiness of life objectively and without pious illusion. The present account has been written out of my enthusiasm for his work and thought.

I am hopeful that the book may attract some who are not already interested in Japanese literature, and for that reason I have included perhaps more background information on Japan than an informed reader would find necessary. The opening chapter provides some biographical information on Ōgai, and the remaining chapters examine his literary work. Such a format seems generally appropriate, but there is of necessity some slight overlapping of information, although not so much, I hope, as to be merely repetitive.

I would like to thank my colleague Professor David Dilworth, whose early interest in Ōgai led me to collaborate with him on a series of translations for UNESCO and eventually to the writing of this book. His advice and his enthusiasm have been invaluable. I also wish to thank

Preface

Mrs. Mary Dilworth for her help in checking over my translations. I am grateful as well to Washington University for a grant provided to help me with the preparation of this manuscript. I am also especially indebted to Roy B. Teele and by Richard Bowring, who read the manuscript most carefully and made many generous suggestions.

J. THOMAS RIMER

St. Louis

An Explanatory Note

Japanese names appear in the Japanese order, family name first: Mori Ōgai, not Ōgai Mori.

Artistic names in common usage are given in the text. Thus: Ōgai, Shōyō (for Tsubouchi Shōyō), Sōseki (for Natsume Sōseki)

For the sake of readers unfamiliar with Japanese, I have referred to Ōgai's works mentioned in the main body of the book by their English titles. Many of the titles are difficult to translate fluently, but even a tentative translation seems a better choice than merely leaving the titles in Japanese.

Following is an alphabetical list of the Japanese titles, with their English equivalents.

"Abe Ichizoku"	The Abe Family
"Asane"	Sleeping Late
"Asobi"	Play
"Chinmoku no tō"	The Tower of Silence
"Chōso Kabe Nobuchika"	Chōso Kabe Nobuchika (a personal name)
"Dokushin"	Living Alone
"Fumizukai"	The Courier
"Fushinchū"	Under Reconstruction
Gan	Wild Goose
"Gyogenki"	Gyogenki (a personal name)
"Hanako"	Hanako (a personal name)
"Hannichi"	Half a Day
"Hebi"	The Snake
"Hōjō Katei"	Hōjō Katei (a personal name)

"Hyaku monogatari"	The Tale of a Hundred Candles
Ikutagawa	The Ikuta River
Izawa Ranken	Izawa Ranken (a personal name)
"Jiisan baasan"	The Old Man and the Old Woman
"Ka no yō ni"	As If
Kaijin	Destruction
Kamen	Masks
"Kanzan Jittoku"	Kanzan Jittoku (personal names)
"Kuriyama Daizen"	Kuriyama Daizen (a personal name)
"Maihime"	The Girl who Danced
"Mōsō"	Delusion
"Munaguruma"	An Empty Cart
"Nagashi"	Back Scrubbing
"Nakajikiri"	From my Ledger
"Nezumizaka"	Rat Hill
Nichiren Shōnin tsuji seppo	The Street Sermon of Nichiren
"Ōgai gyoshi to wa tare zo"	Who is Mori Ōgai?
"Okitsu Yagoemon no isho"	The Last Will and Testament of Okitsu Yagoemon
"Ōshio Heihachirō"	Ōshio Heihachirō (a personal name)
Purumura	Purumula
Omokage	Vestige,
"Sahashi Jingorō"	Sahashi Jingorō (a personal name)
"Saigo no ikku"	The Last Phrase
"Sakai jiken"	The Incident at Sakai
"Sanshō dayū"	Sanshō the Bailiff
Sara no ki	The Sal Tree

An Explanatory Note

Seinen	Youth
Shibue Chūsai	Shibue Chūsai (a personal name)
Shizuka	Shizuka (a personal name)
"Shokudō"	The Dining Room
"Somechigae"	Cloth of Many Colors
"Takasebune"	The Boat on the River Takase
Tama kushige futari Urashima	The Jeweled Casket and the Two Urashimas
"Tenchō"	Heavenly Favor
"Tokō Tahei"	Tokō Tahei (a personal name)
"Tsuge Shirōzaemon"	Tsuge Shirōzaemon (a personal name)
"Tsuina"	Exorcising Demons
"Utakata no ki"	A Record of Froth on the Water
Uta nikki	Poetry Journal
Vita Sexualis	*Vita Sexualis*
"Yasui fujin"	Yasui's Wife
"Yo ga tachiba"	My Point of View
"Yokyō"	Entertainment

Magazine titles have been rendered as follows:

Mannensō	Eternal Grasses
Mezamashigusa	Remarkable Notes
Shiragami zōshi	The Weir
Subaru	The Pleiades

Chronology

1902 Publishes his translation of *The Improvisatore*; marries for the second time; returns to Toyko.

1904 The Russo-Japanese War breaks out; Ōgai sails for the front.

1905 End of hostilities.

1909 Translates *John Gabriel Borkman* of Ibsen for production by Osanai Kaoru; writes *Vita Sexualis* and number of short stories including "Half a Day."

1910 Writes *Youth* and a variety of shorter works, including "Hanako" and "Play."

1911 Writes *Wild Goose* and a number of shorter works.

1912 Begins *Destruction*. After the death of the Emperor Meiji, writes "The Last Will and Testament of Okitsu Yagoemon."

1913 Writes historical accounts, including "The Abe Family," "Sahashi Jingorō," and others; translates *Faust* and *Macbeth*.

1914 Writes more historical works, including "The Incident at Sakai," "Yasui's Wife," and "Sanshō the Bailiff." Translates Hofmannsthal and Strindberg.

1916 Writes *Shibue Chūsai*; resigns from official government positions.

1920 His kidney illness worsens.

1922 Gives up all work because of illness. Dies July 9.

CHAPTER 1

Ōgai's Life

M ORI Ōgai commented on several occasions that he admired both the French novelist Zola and the German Philosopher Eduard von Hartmann for their ability to see "a vast world in a small world." In providing a description of Ōgai's life, the logic must be reversed. Ōgai himself was reticent about many personal details, and Japanese scholars have devoted a considerable amount of effort to piecing together his relationships with other people and to providing information on various matters concerning his professional life as a military doctor and as a writer. Although some of these details remain unclear even today, there is, at the more profound level of Ōgai's creative life, a striking continuity of purpose. His literary works form a spiritual record altogether in accord with his deeper emotional concerns: one illuminates the other. It is best, then, to begin with a brief factual account of Ōgai's life. The meanings and significance of these facts will emerge more clearly when juxtaposed with his writings.

I. *Early Education*

Mori Ōgai was born in 1862, at the very end of the Tokugawa period. He died in 1922, when Japan had become a modern nation with international concerns. His adult life was spent in the intellectual turmoil that grew from the effects on his society of Japan's encounters with the West in international politics, leading to her participation in three wars during his adult lifetime. He was to face the confusions and ambiguities brought about by the

19

introduction of Westren culture into a nation with long
and sophisticated traditions of her own. Indeed, Ōgai's
reactions to these ambiguities have come to epitomize
for later generations the spiritual realities of those times.

Ōgai's birthplace was a small village in the present-day
prefecture of Shimane, on the Japan Sea, where the
daimyō, or Lord of the Tsuwano fief, resided. The area
is a remote one even today, far from the national centers of
culture in Kyoto, the old capital, or Tokyo. Despite this
fact, the *daimyō* was a very progressive-minded man. Ōgai's
father was a physician in his service, and so Ōgai was
permitted to use the private school set up to educate the
children of the important retainers of the Tsuwano family.
His studies were typical of the curriculum at the time:
Confucius and Mencius. "Study" is perhaps a bad description for the process that the children underwent. The texts
of these classics of Chinese philosophy were memorized
in the original Chinese (with some attempt made to help
the students with an artifically devised Japanese pronun-
ciation), and the children repeated, then later wrote out,
the texts without necessarily grasping their meaning. The
effect of what seems like drudgery was sometimes salutary,
for these texts, and the philosophy behind them, usually
remained with the student forever. Indeed, Ōgai learned
to write Chinese beautifully and kept his diaries in that
language. Towards the end of his life, in the midst of
translating Goethe and Ibsen, he continued to compose
poems in classical Chinese structured according to rules
laid down in T'ang China.

Not a great deal has been recorded concerning Ōgai's
early reading in Japanese literature. Late in his life he did
express the fact that he enjoyed the novels and stories
popular at the time.

When I was young, I devoured the books of a lending
library man who used to walk around with books stacked on

his back, in something like a monk's pack. . . . I was first addicted to Bakin, then came to like Kyōden more; but I always preferred Shunsui to Kinsui.[1]

Along with his study of the oriental classics, Ōgai was also tutored in Dutch, the only Western language then taught in Japan. Dutch was considered at that time to be the language of modern medicine, and Ōgai was expected by his father and by the *daimyō* himself to prepare for a career in medicine, with the expectation of following his father. Ōgai did become a physician, but with the coming of the Meiji Restoration, the social structure of the country was completely altered, and the kind of life his father lived was to disappear forever.

The Meiji Restoration, proclaimed in 1868, brought tremendous changes to Japan. The country was opened up to foreign influence, the complex Tokugawa shogunate was disbanded, and the young intelligentsia of the country, a few of whom had been exposed to Europe, began to work toward the creation of a new state that would be modeled partly on the West and that, they were convinced, must exist on a par with the West.

One of the few men already back from Europe at this time was Nishi Amane (1829–1897). Nishi was also a member of the Tswuano clan and was related through his father to Mori Ōgai. Nishi became interested in Dutch studies and managed to visit Holland; when he returned after a considerable amount of observation and study, he became a retainer to the Tokugawa Shogun in 1866. His ideas were sought to help shore up the tottering regime, but two years later, the emperor was on the throne and Nishi joined the government's Department of Military Affairs in Tokyo in 1870. He then began a double career of dedicated scholar and dedicated bureaucrat, writing and teaching the meaning and reality of Western civilization.

In 1872, when Ōgai was ten, he was chosen by the *daimyō* of Tsuwano to go to Tokyo for further training; shortly after his arrival, he went to live in the Nishi household, where he continued his studies in preparation for formal medical training. He also began his study of German, which was by then supplanting Dutch as the language for medical research. Two years later, when he tried to enter the preparatory course for the Tokyo University medical school, he found he was underage and so declared himself two years older, so that by the age of fifteen he was a regular student in medical school. Ōgai's academic record was a good one, and he was considered a promising young man by a number of important friends and teachers.

To be promising in the Japan of the 1870s meant great opportunities and great responsibilities. The young Emperor Meiji in his Charter Oath of 1868 declared that "knowledge shall be sought from all over the world and thus shall be strengthened the foundation of the Imperial polity." A brilliant student might well expect to have an opportunity to go abroad, and at the expense of his government; but then he might also expect to serve the new Meiji state when he returned. When Ōgai himself was chosen, he seemed to have felt no initial reservations, but he spent much of his later adult life trying to reconcile the demands of his inner life with his sense of duty to the state that sent him abroad.

When Ōgai graduated from medical school, in 1881, he made up his mind to make use of his excellent command of German and go abroad. He joined the army with the rank of lieutenant and was soon chosen to visit Germany to make a study of military hygiene. He seemed to be following the pattern set down by his benefactor Nishi Amane. Ōgai left Yokohama in August, 1884, on a French ship bound for Europe and arrived in Berlin on November 11. He remained in Europe until the summer of 1888.

II *Europe and Return*

Berlin brought Ōgai the scientific training that formed the basis for his later military career, but his visit also put him in touch with the finest in nineteenth-century German philosophy and literature, and, in German translation, the great masterpieces of Western literature, from Sophocles to the contemporary French naturalists. Ōgai's diaries show he began a systematic reading of this literature, as well as pursuing his special enthusiasms for Goethe, the *Aesthetics* of Hartmann, and the essays of Schopenhaeur. He later wrote of reading late into the night, filled with the nervous energy of youth. "My nerves are curiously on edge, and although my mind is perfectly calm, I feel irritated merely to open books and follow the path of other people's thoughts. My thoughts, too, begin to move with a life of their own."[2]

Ōgai did not merely study; he traveled to Munich, Dresden, and Leipzig, met distinguished scientists and members of the Saxon royal family, participated in a variety of military maneuvers, and, evidently, had an affair with a German girl that became the subject of several stories. Not a moment of his experience was wasted; he went to the theaters, the museums, the dance halls. And he observed. His diaries, kept in Chinese that served as a kind of shorthand, provide a prodigious record of the places he visited and the people he met. They also served as notes for later works of fiction.

Ōgai was promoted to the rank of captain and returned to Japan, visiting London and Paris before sailing from Marseilles in June, 1888; he reached Tokyo in September, a man now marked by his experiences and ready to act upon them. Ōgai, at twenty-seven, doubtless had the best training in Western literature of any Japanese at the time. Good translations of first-rate Western works were not yet available in Japan (Ōgai later did much to remedy that),

and the brilliant young novelist and scholar of Shakespeare
Tsubouchi Shōyō (1859–1935), Japan's first modern literary
critic, was Ōgai's elder by a mere three years. Shōyō was
well read in English literatⁱre and literary criticism but
never left Japan. Natsume Sōseki, now ranked with Ōgai
as the other great figure in Meiji literature, did not begin
publishing fiction until his own return from England seven-
teen years later. Ōgai knew his own superiority, and he
had no hesitation in attempting to convince others of it.
His superiority in the medical field was also clear. He
was appointed professor of physiology at the Army Medical
School, and he taught anatomy at the Tokyo Academy of
Fine Arts as well.

In the years before 1894, when Ōgai left his work in
Tokyo to serve in the Sino-Japanese war, he consolidated
the intellectual substance of his European experience. In
1889 Ōgai began a literary magazine, *Shiragami zōshi*
(The Weir), that carried both his own contributions and
those of other writers interested in the creation of a
modern literature. The magazine gave him an outlet to
develop his own critical ideas and his personal sense of
a literary *métier*. His contributions often included translations (Washington Irving, Bret Harte, Lessing, E. T. A.
Hoffman, Tolstoi, Kleist, and others), as well as original
critical pieces.

Ōgai's most important activity at the time was probably
his work done in translating European poetry into Japanese
for a collection published in 1889 entitled *Omokage*
(Vestiges), in which he and a number of other gifted
young writers worked out the first effective translations
of works by such poets as Shakespeare, Heine, Goethe,
and Byron. The traditional *haiku* and *waka* were still the
major Japanese poetic forms of the day, and the early
and tentative translations of Western poetry that had
preceded *Vestiges* had of necessity transposed the originals
into something close to a Japanese poetic diction. An 1882

translation of Gray's "Elegy," for example, changed the original:

> The curfew tolls the knell of parting day,
>   The lowing herd wind slowly o'er the lea,
> The plowman homeward plods his weary way,
>   And leaves the world to darkness and to me.

to:

> The mountains are misty,
> And, as the evening
> Bell sounds,
> The oxen in the lea
> Slowly walk
> Returning home.
> The plowman too
> Is weary and
> At last departs;
> I alone
> In the twilight hour
> Remain behind.[3]

Ōgai's unsigned translations in *Vestiges* are generally thought to include Mignon's song from *Wilhelm Meister* and Ophelia's song from *Hamlet,* among others. The poetic diction created here by Ōgai became a model for the young Japanese poets; poems in the "new style" became a highly acceptable form of expression after the publication of the collection. *Vestiges* sold well; so well, in fact, that the fees provided Ōgai permitted him to finance the publication of *The Weir.*

Ōgai was married in 1889 to Akamatsu Toshiko, the daughter of a colleague of his benefactor Nishi Amane, who acted as official go-between. The marriage was unsuccessful, although a son was born to the couple. Ōgai divorced his wife a year later, in 1890. He never alluded in any of his writings to the reasons for the divorce. A

traditional Japanese arranged marriage may well have
seemed repugnant to a man who had tasted the freer
life of European society. His first works of fiction, all of
them set in Germany, call for a freedom in love that
seemed denied him. It was also at this time that he began
a translation of Hans Christian Andersen's *The Improvisatore,* that highly romantic and psychologically acute novel
whose hero so much resembled Ōgai in certain facets of
his temperament.

In 1894, hostilities broke out with China, and Ōgai,
assigned important medical duties, sailed for Korea; as
a result, his literary journal, and a medical journal he
founded as well, were suspended. Ōgai kept notebooks
of his day-to-day military activities but wrote nothing
substantial about his experiences. He returned to Tokyo
the following year and resumed his position as head of
the Army Medical School. He began a second literary
journal, *Mezamashigusa* (Remarkable Notes). Although
Ōgai continued to use this new magazine as a forum for
his own ideas, he attracted a number of leading critics and
writers who also used it as a form for significant contributions. The magazine continued until 1902, but when Ōgai
was transferred to Kokura, on the southern island of
Kyushu, in 1899, he lost close touch with the literary world
that was centered in Tokyo, and *Remarkable Notes* soon
lost its role as a kind of avant-garde forum for intellectuals.
The journal was later absorbed by other publications.

Ōgai's new military assignment in Kokura, a small city of
no contemporary cultural significance, marked a complete
and devastating change in his life. Until then he had
been in the center of Japanese artistic and scientific circles,
prodding and pushing them toward a vision of modernity
and progress he knew to be the right one. Energy, and a
related arrogance, might bring some success in the artistic
field, but such attitudes were dangerous for an officer in
the army to harbor. His transfer was intended as a purpose-

ful reprimand to a man who complained too much and insisted too much on modern views of medicine that were difficult if not impossible for older officers trained in traditional methods to grasp. In 1899, at thirty-six, Ōgai found himself banished from everything he felt important. The shock was enormous, and it brought from him, at thirty-nine, his first confession of faith as a writer, discreet and guarded though it was.

In 1900 a friend and writer on a local newspaper asked Ōgai, then in the midst of his "exile" in Kokura, to describe himself to his readers, and in his essay "Ōgai gyoshi to wa tare zo" (Who is Mori Ōgai?) he attempted to tell them. These difficult years when his busy Tokyo career seemed at an end were the cause for considerable reflection on Ōgai's part, and he reminded his readers that he was basically a doctor and a military man, and that in fact, although he was referred to as a novelist, he had written only a few stories that might qualify him in any way to be considered a writer. Ōgai's view of himself was in fact quite accurate, since, with the exception of the three short stories based on his German experiences, and one short imitation of the Tokugawa novelist Ihara Saikaku, a story of the gay quarters entitled "Somechigae" (Cloth of Many Colors), Ōgai had only prepared translations or written about literature. Looking back from the vantage point of his later career, his comment may seem an understatement, but Ōgai's important writings were done mostly in his late forties and fifties. In 1900, a real artistic career still seemed tenuous to him.

Writing, stated Ōgai, is communication with fellow human beings; coming to Kokura and relinquishing the literary world of Tokyo meant that in effect Mori Ōgai died. Only a few rocks of criticism had been thrown on his grave since then, but his critics were shouting down a ghost who was no more. Ōgai may be dead, he continued, but

... I am the same as I was before. And indeed I am not merely
what I was before. I have studied and learned since that time.
I may move along like the limp tortoise of Chinese legend,
but I have made the best of every day. It is in this I quietly
place my faith.[4]

Quiet reading and reflection, he suggested had produced
a not-altogether disgruntled calm, and the reading of
contemporary European works (he mentioned in particular
Hauptmann) continued to stimulate him enormously. A new
generation of Japanese writers coming to the fore, Ōgai
concluded, might be described as *epigonoi* ("born after");
second-rate they might be when compared to the early
pioneers of modern Japanese literature, but the new Ōgai
would join them.

Ōgai remained in Kokura until 1902 and produced little
during those silent "years of exile" as he called them. Yet
that period was the turning point for his later artistic
development, for his attitude changed from a combativeness
to a kind of positive resignation. He seemed to be grasping
a necessary sense of his own limitations. Those quiet years
were actually put to good use; he made a closer study of
German aesthetic theory, finished his translation of Andersen's lengthy novel, and began taking an interest in the
great feudal families of Kyushu, about which he was to
write in such detail during the end of his life.

Ōgai made one trip to Tokyo early in 1902, for his second
marriage. The bride was the twenty-three year old Araki
Shigé. He had remained single for eleven years. His new
bride was chosen for him by his mother Mineko, a strong-
minded woman to whom her son was emotionally beholden
all his life, in one way or another. Shigé, who suffered
through an unsuccessful first marriage herself, was a beautiful woman with a will of her own. Ōgai, who had stated
on more than one occasion that he would be just as happy
without re-marrying, seemingly found the first period of
their life together a trying one, if his story "Half a Day" can

serve as any indication. Shigé herself had aspirations to become a writer, and Ōgai later arranged for the publication
of her fictionalized version of her first marriage. She also
published an account of her troubles with Ōgai, and the
emotional demands of her own artistic temperament made
their life together difficult.

The couple returned briefly to Kokura; then Ōgai was
permanently recalled by his military superiors, and they
were able to return to Tokyo, where they moved in with
his mother. (Perhaps the move was a major cause of
the subsequent troubles between them.) Whatever the
ultimate nature of the relations between Ōgai and Shigé,
she bore him a number of children, and he seems to have
been a devoted and conscientious father to them. Shigé
outlived her husband, dying in 1936.

Ōgai's return to Tokyo was, in effect, a reprieve from
the army. Restored to positions of importance (By 1907
he was appointed Director of the Bureau of Medical Affairs
for the War Bureau.), he commanded great prestige in his
professional career. In 1902, at forty, he began his mature
life as a writer, scholar, and government bureaucrat.

Yet all he did was marked from that time on by a sense
of irony and detachment that seemed to form a stronger
and stronger element in his character. The failure of his
first marriage, his years in Kokura, and the early troubles
with his second wife may have contributed to this growing
air of objectivity and aristocratic disdain (sometimes char-
acterized, I think incorrectly, as emotional fatigue); on
the other hand, elements of such attitudes occur even in
his earliest works. Certainly those attitudes were intensified
in the decade that closed with the death of the Emperor
Meiji in 1912.

III *Full Maturity*

By the time Ōgai returned to Tokyo, he had become
aware of the modern movement in European literature.

During his visit to Germany he had absorbed German romanticism; now he became aware of Ibsen, Strindberg, Rilke, and Hofmannsthal. His own scientific training and personal temperament (as well as the situation he found in his own society) made him feel closer in spirit to these men than to the romantics. Ōgai began to translate their works and to study and experiment with the forms in which they chose to write, poetry and drama.

Much of this experimentation involved an attempt to develop a modern literary language sufficiently flexible to sustain the kind of psychological insights Ōgai wished to convey. Classical Japanese, still in use for literary works in the early Meiji period, had centuries before moved a considerable distance from ordinary speech. Classical Chinese, much studied during the preceding Tokugawa period, had also influenced the language of literary prose by serving as a source of difficult compounds and constructions far removed from the vernacular. Successful attempts had been made, of course, to write a form of contemporary Japanese in certain popular books on the Tokugawa period, but such works were considered without literary merit, vulgar comic books for the semiliterate. To some extent, in fact, such charges were correct.

By the 1880s, however, a number of young Japanese writers who had learned something of Western literature came to realize that to describe in their own work the kind of contemporary psychological human reactions they admired in Western literature would require a prose that took into account the vernacular language. The artistic problems were rendered more difficult by the fact that even spoken Japanese at that time was not yet standardized; the Tokyo dialect had not yet gained supremacy as the national language, and new words and constructions were being coined at a rapid rate to express ideas and concepts hitherto unknown in Japanese.[5] Ōgai remarked in his 1915 story "Saigo no ikku" (The Last Phrase) that ". . . officials of the Tokugawa family had no idea of the Western word 'martyr' nor was the word 'self-sacrifice' in the dictionaries at the time."[6] He might well have gone on to explain that there were hundreds of other common words unavailable in his own dictionaries when he was a young man.

Ōgai's early stories used the traditional vocabulary available to him; now his experiments in drama and poetry made possible the rapid development of both forms in Japan after 1900. In addition to his stylistic contributions, Ōgai's efforts toward the creation of a modern theater in Japan, through his translation of Ibsen and other modern dramatists and through the writing of his own experimental plays, were of great historical importance. His talents as a dramatist, indeed, were more apparent with each short play he wrote, and he might have made a major contribution early in the decade if he had not gone off to war again in 1904.

Ōgai's departure for the front forced the cancellation of other projects as well. In 1902 he and Ueda Bin (1874–1916), the distinguished poet and translator from the French, began a journal, *Mannensō* (Eternal Grasses), to publish works on aesthetics and poetry. Ōgai contributed a number of articles and doubtless saw the magazine as a forum to replace *The Weir*, but with his departure from Tokyo, the magazine ceased publication.

The Russo-Japanese War of 1904–1905 was a more complex experience for the Japanese than the Sino-Japanese War a decade before. If the intellectuals had welcomed the earlier confrontation, they now felt some conflict of values, and the economic and social strains created by the war effort brought the first strong feelings of ambiguity about the direction of Japan's national destiny. Ōgai had written nothing about the Sino-Japanese War ten years before, but he composed a considerable amount of poetry during the Russo-Japanese War, and his visit to Manchuria produced a satirical sketch of military life, "Asane" (Sleeping Late).

Back in Tokyo in 1906, after the end of hostilities, Ōgai continued to pursue his new interest in poetry and his former concern with modernizing the theater. He and his colleague Kako Tsurudo (1855–1931), whose strong interest was in Chinese poetry and in reforming the traditional *waka*, began a poetry journal, and Ōgai took an active interest in encouraging a large circle of younger poets. He also began the systematic translation of a series of important modern plays for production. Ōgai's real contributions to the modern theater, however, began in 1909, when the young producer Osanai Kaoru (1881–1928) staged Ōgai's translation of Ibsen's *John Gabriel Borkman*, the first proper attempt to mount a modern play in Japan. (The opening night of that production, one of the great events in the cultural history of Meiji Japan, is chronicled in Ōgai's novel *Seinen* (Youth), written the following year). He then translated a number of other plays for production and composed his own best work for the theater.

If Ōgai's dramas and poetry were experiments in the creation of new forms in Japanese literature, his prose works of the period represented finished creations of a high artistic standard. In a series of stories and novels, Ōgai turned his attention to the growing complexities of late Meiji society. The journal, *Subaru* (The Pleiades), begun in 1909 and the most prestigious of all the publications he helped edit, was an important outlet for a number of his most provocative essays and stories. Ōgai's sense of social malaise lay behind much of the best work he wrote during these years, and his complex attitudes toward contemporary society called forth one particularly revealing essay in which he attempted to characterize his own psychology.

In 1909, Ōgai was asked to write a short article on his attitudes toward life and the result, *Yo ga tachiba* (My Point of View), seems in many ways a startling document from a man in the midst of translating Ibsen, Wilde, and Rilke, as well as writing an important novel of his own, *Vita Sexualis,* half-a-dozen short stories, to say nothing of a long and carefully researched biography of King Asoka and the beginnings of Indian Buddhism composed in collaboration with Ōmura Seigai (1868–1927), a well-known historian of Asian art and culture at the time. Yet the mind exists in layers, and Ōgai's detachment from his own considerable activity may help to suggest something of the enormous complexity of his emotional responses.

Ōgai begins by recognizing the fact that others have found him discontented and sarcastic, which he denies; writers cannot be lined up and judged like schoolboys. He writes according to his own personality, Ōgai continues, and if others are "better," that fact must remain a matter of indifference to him. His real attitude might be best expressed in a term he found difficult to express in Japanese, one of *resignation.*

I do not merely use this term in relation to the contemporary literary world; I feel this way about every phase of human society. Others may say that such an attitude suggests I am undergoing some kind of spiritual agony, but on the contrary, I am perfectly serene. Perhaps such an attitude suggests a lack of self-respect. On this point as well, however, I have no apologies to make.[7]

Ōgai's criticism reflects on himself, but it reflects as well on the increasing sense of alienation felt by the intellectuals from the aims of the Meiji state. Natsume Sōseki, in his splendid novel *Sore kara* (And Then), written in the same years as Ōgai's essay, states the problem in a discussion between the protagonist Daisuke and a friend.

. . . look at Japan. She is the kind of country that can't survive unless she borrows money from the West. In spite of this, she tries to play the role of a first-class power, she tries to force her way into the company of the first-class powers. . . . She is like a frog trying to be as big as a cow. Of course she will soon burst. This struggle affects you and me, and everybody else. Because of the pressure of competition with the West, the Japanese have no time to relax and think and do something worthwhile. They are brought up in an atmosphere of tension and frugality and then are made to engage in furious activity. No wonder they are all neurotics. Talk to them, you will find they are all fools. They think of nothing except themselves and their immediate needs.[8]

Ōgai's own attitudes, given his point of view, seem almost inevitable. The close and dialectical relationship between definitions of self and society illustrated in so many of his works gives a contemporary, and a disturbing aspect to much of his writing; the restless emptiness suffered by many of Ōgai's characters is a recognizable phenomenon in modern literature around the world. In Japan at this period, there were particular problems of great social and moral concern, many of them long-range effects of the Russo-Japanese war. Workers, underpaid, took up an interest in socialist doctrine, and the government reacted by taking repressive measures, many of them occasioned by the so-called Kōtoku Shūsui Incident in 1911, when Shūsui (1871–1911), a prominent and in fact a quite distinguished figure in leftist political circles, was implicated in what was presumed to be a plot to assassinate the Emperor Meiji. He was executed. The brutal incident was profoundly upsetting to Meiji intellectuals, the final end to their political innocence. Ōgai, even though a high functionary himself, reacted to the growing air of stagnation and repression that he found typical of the government. The final shock, however, came a year later, with the death of the Emperor Meiji.

IV The Final Years

The Emperor Meiji stood much larger than life in the eyes of the Japanese; he seemed to stand as a symbol of the progress of the country and served as a rallying point around whom the nation could unite, from a period in the 1860s (in Ōgai's childhood) when the country was threatened, like China, with invasion from without, to a period in the early twentieth century when she stood by treaty and treatment alike as the most powerful nation in Asia. Yet Japan's international coming of age in the twentieth century had brought her all the familiar difficulties as well: industrial poverty, social discontent, and intellectual alienation. The death of the emperor, who had presided over an era of progress, brought a terrible loss of confidence to the country. The death of the emperor was immediately followed by a sensational incident, the ritual suicide of General Nogi Maresuke (1849–1912), the great hero of the Russo-Japanese War, who wished to follow his master to death in the old samurai tradition. A number of the important writers in Japan responded to this incident. The suicide forms part of the theme of *Kokoro,* the celebrated novel by Ōgai's contemporary Natsume Sōseki, who treated the General's death as a somber pavane running in counterpoint to the main events of the narrative. Akutakawa Ryūnosuke, on the other hand, composed a withering attack on the old morality in his short story "The General."

Nogi's suicide marked another turning point in Ōgai's artistic work as well. Shortly afterward he published a brief account entitled "Okitsu Yogoemon no isho" (The Last Will and Testament of Okitsu Yogoemon), based on a historical incident. Ōgai here rendered the emotional state of a retainer about to commit ritual suicide. Ōgai followed this story a year later with "Abe Ichizoku" (The Abe Family), another account, based on historical records, of suicide, but written from an objective point of view and, by implication at least, more critical of the practice.

Ōgai now pursued a double literary career. In Western literature, he continued to devote his enormous energies in this last decade of his life to translations of the best, and often the newest, that European literature had to offer. He produced Japanese versions of Ibsen, Gorki, Rilke, Hofmannsthal's *Oedipus and the Sphinx*, as well as acting versions of several plays of Strindberg for production by Osanai. Above and beyond this, however, he had two major interests in foreign literature at this period. The first was Shakespeare. Ōgai spent an enormous amount of effort translating *Macbeth*, a play he greatly admired, in 1913 for a stage production. Still more important was his attraction to Goethe. Ōgai translated first the play of Goethe's youthful genius, *Götz von Berlichingen* and followed it with an extraordinary labor of love and scholarship, a complete translation of *Faust*. He also wrote a biography of Goethe, based on German sources.

In his own writing, Ōgai turned more and more to historical themes, and a considerable number (but by no means all) of his works written until his death draw on Japanese history, or occasionally on Chinese history, for their background. Meticulously researched and carefully written, these last works show Ōgai at his best as an artist and as a man, largely because of the ability he found within himself, in the full maturity of his thought, to transcend the limitations of his time to seek a dispassionate and humane objectivity. Ōgai provided the first statement concerning his attitude in an essay composed to explain the methods of composition used in creating his short novel, "Sanshō dayū" (Sanshō the Bailiff).

A number of my friends say that other writers choose their material and treat it on an emotional basis, while I do so on a rational one. Yet I hold this to be true of all my literary work, not merely of the stories based on historical characters. In general, I would say that my works are not "Dionysian" but rather "Apollonian." I have never exerted the kind of effort required to make a story "Dionysian." And indeed, if I were able to expend a comparable effort, it would be an effort to make my creation all the more contemplative.[9]

Borrowing his metaphor from Nietzsche, Ōgai seems to be describing a battle won in himself, a battle over his own emotions, disappointments, even over his own sense of "resignation." The balance gained from this hard-won calm was to sustain him for the last years of his life.

Yet this serenity was not mere sweetness without depth. In an essay written the following year entitled "Munaguruma" (An Empty Cart), Ōgai included an extraordinary passage in which he suggests a parable with his own life. The essay proper deals with the phrase "empty cart" and discusses the methods needed to define and use this old word properly in contemporary language: how, in short, to use the past in the present. As Ōgai proceeds, he describes the associations the word has collected in his own mind. He imagines watching the cart.

... because the cart is empty, its enormous size is all the more striking. The huge cart as it comes along makes the wide road seem narrow. The horses tied to the cart are sturdy and well-nourished. They move along in an easy fashion as though they had forgotten they were tied to it. The man leading the horses is a big man, who stands tall. He walks along with great strides, as if he were the very soul of this stout horse, this huge cart. This man never wavers. When he encounters something, he never slackens his step, nor does he go faster. The word "arrogant" might well have been created just to describe him.

Those who walk move away when the cart comes. Those on horseback as well. The carts of the nobility veer away. The vehicles of the wealthy avoid it. The soldiers break rank before it. The funeral processions make way. In the track of the cart, even the streetcar conductor must stop and await its passing.

Yet this is merely one empty cart.

Each time I see the coming of the cart, I cannot restrain myself from looking for it and from watching it pass by. And yet it never occurs to me that the cart should be loaded with anything to carry. When I compare this cart with one that has been loaded, I hardly need debate which is superior to the other. Even if the loaded cart is piled with valuables.[10]

The powerful images conjured up here suggest, as a number of Japanese scholars have pointed out, the responses of a man who is looking back on his life with a freedom gained from a disassociation from public life, from conventional wisdom, even his own, from all the "freight of the world." Yet the ambiguous poetry of the statement does not conceal the efforts that led Ōgai to his final position of serenity; and the man who walks at his divine right pace is still an ideal and no mirror image of the author.

Ōgai's final comments of his life and work came one year later, in the 1916 essay "Nakajikiri" (From My Ledger), in which he looks back with a certain asperity on his various activities: in none of his endeavors—novelist, playwright, poet, historian, philosopher—did Ōgai feel he had succeeded. In fact, he wrote that he had no real intention to set out to be any of those things, "yet the opportunities come, and one writes." He realized that he thus was open to the charge of being a dilettante. Nevertheless, what is past is past; now he is retired, a man of leisure, a child with his toys. What kind of toys did he play with?

I am reading books. The old Chinese classics. For modern Western works are hard to come by, and those I am able to occasionally obtain deal with the war in Europe. This is my receptive side. Yet as for my *productivity*, my remaining energy as a writer only permits me to continue composing lyric poetry and history. My *vita minima* I carry on.[11]

Ōgai's *vita minima*, in fact, seems to have reduced him to the classic definition of literature in the East: poetry and historical writing. "From My Ledger" is dotted with references to Chinese writers, some of them fairly obscure. Yet there are also references to Zola and other Western writers, and in speaking of neo-Confucianism he makes comparisons with Schopenhauer.

The tonality of the essay suggests a wise old man, subdued and reflective. Ōgai may have suffered deeply at this time. His mother died in 1916, and her loss after their close and complex relationship may have strengthened his sense of withdrawal. Nevertheless, Ōgai was only fifty-five when he wrote the essay. In that same year he wrote a number of his finest historical stories and published his masterpiece *Shibue Chūsai,* the recreation of the life of a doctor who lived in the preceding Tokugawa period.

These last confessions, cast in the form of informal essays, become a form of art themselves. The man is seen, but through a framework of his own design. Ōgai's personality lies far beneath his most personal statements, just as his own human experience lies somewhere beneath his fiction. This many-layered effect accounts for much of the irony and astringency that mark a large portion of his writing. Indeed, the great humanitarian sentiments reflected in his best works usually occur on those artistic occasions when Ōgai is furthest from his immediate experience, writing from a model outside himself. An examination of the ambiguities and complexities of Ōgai's personal relationships with his mother, wives, children, and the women he may have known in Germany or during his long period of bachelorhood after the end of his first marriage may help reveal his personality but risks deflecting efforts to properly evaluate the literary works themselves, which must be read as expansions from his human experiences rather than as sample pages from a case history. Ōgai's best work can be set quite apart from his career and still retain its pungency and evocative power; in particular the last stories hold up questions to society that penetrate deeply into the meaning of contemporary experience so apparent to Ōgai by the time of the First World War (in which Japan was involved, even to the extent of sending troops into Russia).

These last stories seem less a retreat into history, as some critics have asserted, than the throwing up of a moral framework strong enough to weather the storms.

About the time of the composition of *Shibue Chūsai,* when Ōgai was fifty-five, he resigned from a number of official positions and was named as a curator for the Imperial Household Museum. During his last few years, Ōgai suffered from a kidney disease, and he died in 1922, at the age of sixty-one.

CHAPTER 2

The Years of Apprenticeship, 1890–1902

MORI Ōgai was a prolific writer, and his experiments led him to express himself in virtually every literary form available to him during the period of his creative life, from poetry in Chinese to modern drama. Experiment suggests progression, and there is in his work a steady and cumulative development of certain central themes and concerns that imposed a consistency of design, if a design in momentum, on his work. Whatever the dangers of examining a writer's work in terms of chronological development, the adoption of such a method for Ōgai is the most satisfactory approach. Yet, as I suggested above, there is a danger in reading these works as disguised autobiography. Ōgai's reflections of his themes, not the events depicted, are the basis of his art; as a result, even his slight pieces possess an objectivity and a moral weight unusual in modern Japanese literature.

Another way to trace the development of Ōgai's concerns is to take careful note of the works he translated. A comparison between his own writing and the works of European literature that he translated at the same time often suggests a startling similarity of concern. This does not mean that Ōgai's works are variations or copies of European models. Far from it; in fact there is usually no superficial resemblance at all. Rather, Ōgai, when faced with an intellectual or moral concern, seemed to come to terms with his own position both by reading and translating European authors

41

he respected who were responding to a similar challenge and by working out his own stance in his own fashion, through his own literary means—poem, novel, or story. For this reason I have discussed Ōgai's translations when his interest in a particular author seems to shed light on his own writing.

I Ōgai's "Romantic Period"

The first period of Ōgai's creative life as a writer, from 1889 to 1894, shortly after his return from Germany in 1888, is often referred to as his "romantic period." During this time he wrote and published three tales about Germany. These early works, although somewhat atypical of his later compositions, have remained among his most popular. Ōgai was still a young man (twenty-six in 1889) and these stories represent his youthful point of view, although their general excellence of style does not suggest the work of a beginner.

Ōgai evidently had a love affair in Germany, for shortly after his return to Tokyo, a German girl arrived by ship in Yokohama in search of him and was only with difficulty persuaded to return to Europe by friends and members of his family. Some of these incidents are described in a circumscribed way in a later story, "Fushinchū" (Under Reconstruction), written in 1910. Ōgai was soon given a wife chosen for him by his family, in the traditional fashion, but divorced her a year later. Against this background of an unhappy present Ōgai wrote these three adventures, and a close perusal of his German diaries shows that he made use of his own experiences in creating the people and events that appear in these narratives.

The first of these stories, "Maihime" (The Girl Who Danced, 1890), has often been cited as the first great piece of modern short-fiction writing in Japan. Modern the story certainly is, in terms of its frank psychology and skillful observation of human weakness, but in style it owes more to the elegant traditions of written classical Japanese. The enormously gifted novelist Futabatei Shimei published the first part of his novel *Ukigumo,* the first work written in the modern vernacular, only the year before. Ōgai read it later and recorded that he was tremendously impressed by Shimei's achievements; but he had not chosen to make "The Girl Who Danced" the vehicle for any linguistic experiments. To a modern reader, there seems to be a discrepancy in the Japanese text between the formal quality of the vocabulary and sentence structure and the penetrating contemporary nature of the narration. Even the Japanese title, "Maihime," an old Japanese term that might have suited the vocabulary of *The Tale of Genji,* seems archaic and too aristocratic for his model, a dancer in a German theater troupe. On the other hand, there is no denying that the use of such vocabulary lends dignity to Ōgai's account.

"The Girl Who Danced" tells the story, in the first person, of a young man, Ota Toyotarō, who is sent to Berlin by the Japanese government for a program of study. There by chance he meets and befriends a young girl named Alice, and, despite a severe upbraiding by his superiors, he begins living with her. Ota watches the inevitable development of her feelings and her sensibilities; as his involvement with her deepens, he rejects his program of study and becomes a journalist. Eventually, however, Ota is taken to task for his actions by a Japanese friend, Aizawa Kenkichi. Aizawa introduces him to a Japanese nobleman, who, intrigued by Ota's knowledge of Germany, hires him as his private secretary. The pair convince Ota that his ultimate duties do not lie in self-seeking (i.e., living with Alice) but in serving his nation. "I was tricked," Ota comments, for the count "appealed to my desire to excel." Alice now expects a child, but Ota cannot bring himself to refuse the count's insistence that he return to Japan. Wandering in a snowstorm while trying to think how to tell Alice of his resolution, Ota finally arrives at her apartment and collapses in a delirious fever. Alice goes mad and Ota, crushed spiritually, eventually returns to Japan.

Melodramatic in outline, the text, lyrical and mordantly ironic by turns, is an astonishing first work, almost a total success. The exotic quality of the narrative certainly must have impressed its first readers; from a contemporary point of view, however, the real success of the story seems to be in the grasp Ōgai has on the ambiguous nature of duty. "The Girl Who Danced" is less a love story than the memoir of a man who has renounced love and who tries to come to terms with his own weakness.

. . . while I was repudiating authority, something still troubled me. I was now annoyed that I had been following a road others had mapped out for me. But I was still afraid of failing to meet their expectations. I now despised them for driving me, but the thought of displeasing them still frightened me. I could not stop oscillating between freedom and subservience. While I was trying to assert myself in Berlin and break free of the tradition that had bound me, I kept thinking of something that happened to me when I set sail for Yokohama. I walked up the gangplank as though I were a shining hero, knowing that my superiors were watching me and that my mother was among them. But once the ship got under way I wept like a child. And while I was in Berlin I began to realize that I lacked as much courage as my convictions demanded of me.[1]

Given such self-knowledge on Ota's part, the final lines of the story seem inevitable and, in terms of the general thrust of Ōagi's theme, carry an enormous freight.

Until the day I left her, I repeatedly embraced her and cried over her, knowing that each day there was less life in her. At last I left Berlin and started back to Japan.

The Count, Aizawa, and I arranged to provide Alice and the child with a small annuity. I know that Aizawa Kenkichi only wanted to help me, but I shall hate him until I die.[2]

Ota, the protagonist of "The Girl Who Danced," was the chief actor in the happenings recounted there. In Ōgai's second tale "Utakata no ki" (a rather lyrical title that might be rendered as "A Record of Froth on the Water"), the Japanese protagonist, an art student named Kose, is a bystander. The theme is again madness and death, but this time Ōgai aimed higher and experimented with at least partial success in combining two levels of plot: the madness and death of Ludwig II of Bavaria (1845–1886) is described in parallel with the death of Ōgai's heroine Marie.

Kose meets Marie at a café in Munich frequented by artists. He recognizes this girl of twenty as the child he had seen selling violets and had helped six years before. Marie kisses him on the forehead and, angry at the laughter and commotion made by the other art students, leaves the café. Kose then learns from a German friend that she is a model at the art school and many think her slightly deranged. On his part Kose has been haunted by the memory of the child he saw selling flowers six years before and has tried to capture his remembered impressions in a painting of the Lorelei. When Marie visits his studio, she sees the painting and tells him of her past life.

Marie's father was a painter admired by Ludwig II, who on one occasion had tried to make love to her mother; in fact, Marie suggests, this unfortunate incident may represent the first sign of the king's madness, and he evidently still calls out for "Marie." (Both mother and daughter have the same name.) Marie goes on to tell Kose that after her father's death, she suffered various vicissitudes before being taken in by a fishing family living on the shores of Lake Starnberg, near Munich. Eventually she became a model at the art school.

Marie and Kose decide to visit the lake to see the spot where she lived as a child. In the course of their journey, they learn that Ludwig is at the lake also, in his chateau, surrounded by his doctors. On a carriage ride at the lake, the two become more intimate. They rent a boat and row along the bank, where they see the king and his doctor. Spotting the couple in the boat, the king shouts "Marie!" walks into the water, and drowns. Marie faints, falls out of the boat, and drowns as well. Kose takes her body to a fisherman's hut that turns out to be the simple home of the family with whom she lived. Marie cannot be revived, and Kose can only lament the tragedy of a life that vanishes like foam on the water. The story concludes with an account of the elaborate funeral held for King Ludwig; in contrast, only Kose, kneeling before his unfinished painting of the Lorelei, remembers the death of the girl.

A more complex experiment, the story may fail to achieve a perfect union between its obviously disparate elements, but emotionally it presents a rather satisfying whole. Ōgai's explanation of the death of the king is purely fanciful (the details remain unknown even now) yet inoffensive. Indeed Ōgai mentioned in a later essay that while he was in Germany he read a number of speculative stories on the subject, and that there was even a play staged on the theme; there is a suggestion in what Ōgai wrote that he felt a desire to improve on what he had read.

The events in the story concerning the attraction between Kose and Marie were based on the relationship between a friend of Ōgai's in Germany, the painter Harada Naojirō (1863–1899) and a German woman named Marie Huber. Nevertheless, the construction of the story represents more an idealized portrait of the heroine than the account of any actual relationship. The Marie of the story, likened to the classical goddess Minerva, is a figure of romance and tragedy, a wise and inspired figure who seems through her very instability to have understood the deep meanings of life and art. In this sense, there is a certain resonance between her death and that of the mad king. As noted above, a year before the story Ōgai had published his beautiful translation of Ophelia's mad song from *Hamlet* and there seems more than a casual similarity between Shakespeare's images recast in Japanese and Ōgai's description of the sad and lyrical death of Marie. The heightened romantic atmosphere of the text also resembles in its high emotional pitch the technique shown in the stories of Kleist in which Ōgai took a great interest at this time. His translations of two of them, "The Earthquake in Chili" and "The Betrothal in Santo Domingo" appeared in print about this time. Alice's madness, in "The Girl Who Danced," came from a breakdown in physical and moral health; Marie's malaise, as well as her insight into the wellsprings of life and art, are deeper.

In Ōgai's third and last story set abroad, "Fumizukai" (The Courier), published in 1891, the framework remains the same: a Japanese bystander witnesses a European woman in a tragic situation. Kobayashi, a Japanese military officer on duty in Germany, meets Ida, the daughter of a nobleman. She is a fine musician and is engaged to Kobayashi's German colleague Meerheim. Kobayashi finds her most attractive, and she finds in him a friend whom she can trust and so sends him off with a letter for her aunt in Dresden. Not until sometime later does Kobayashi learn that in order to avoid a marriage she found distasteful, she decided to become a lady-in-waiting to the queen. "I thought of a solution," Ida told him. "I would go to the palace which, like the Roman Catholic Church, understands rituals but not compassion, and let that become my tomb." The letter requesting the appointment was the letter with which Kobayashi was entrusted.

In "The Courier" the state of tension between self-fulfillment and duty has been shifted from the Japanese student to the German heroine, but they resemble each other in the conflict they feel between a strong desire for self-assertion and an equally powerful compulsion to retreat. Ida gives up her own creative expressiveness, her music, in which she was so skillful that she could deeply

move others (there is a little shepherd boy who plays the
flute for her; when she leaves, the boy, abandoned by his
private Muse, commits suicide.) She abandons her own
chance at personal fulfillment through art just as Toyotarō
abandons his freedom by leaving Europe. Although Alice
was a dancer, both Marie and Ida seem in touch with
greater and more dangerous powers of creativity. Although
the emotional scope encompassed in "The Courier" is more
restricted than that in "A Record of Froth on the Water,"
this last story is for that reason a more restrained and
perfect piece of writing.

Ōgai's homage in these early works to the European
culture he learned to love during his visit to Germany is
sincere, and his debt to German romanticism is great.
Nevertheless the stories rise above mere imitations because
the rebelliousness in Ōgai's mind against his own culture
was genuine. There is ambiguity expressed as well, for both
Toyotarō and Ida show that at least part of personal fulfillment must involve submission to duty. Here the theme
appears amid the trappings of European exoticism; in
Ōgai's last period he was able to expand the same ambiguity
into the powerful statements found in his last tales. In these
three early stories, however, the tension is shown between
submission and the freedom (that can lead even to madness) known by the creative person. The later stories penetrate much deeper and come fully from circumstances conceived of within Ōgai's own culture.

II　*Ōgai's Translation of* The Improvisatore

Ōgai's second tribute to his years in Germany was the
painstaking work he did in preparing a translation into
Japanese of an effective and surprisingly sophisticated novel
by Hans Christian Andersen, *The Improvisatore,* written
in 1835. Ōgai's translation was made from a German version
by H. Denhardt.

Ōgai began his translation in 1892 and he worked on it for nine years. When the full translation was published, Ōgai's belief in the book was shown to be well-founded; Andersen's novel had a tremendous effect on younger writers and on the general reading public. In the course of making his translation, Ōgai managed to solve a number of problems pertaining to the modernization of the Japanese language too complex to discuss here, but, more important perhaps, he found in the protagonist of Andersen's novel a model for his own developing sensibility and a reflection of many of his own attitudes.

The Improvisatore is no longer remembered outside of Denmark, but Andersen's novel was much admired and imitated everywhere in the latter part of the nineteenth century.

The story, told in the first person, relates the various adventures of a poor young Italian who has great talent as a poet and can improvise verse on a given subject; a poor young man, he falls in love with an opera singer, Annunciata, and, in a duel for her affections, wounds his friend Bernardo and flees Rome. After a number of colorful adventures during which he comes to understand the ambiguity of all human relationships, he returns to the wealthy family that offered to help him, suppresses his natural gifts for poetry, and studies to be an Abbé.

Even this bare summary immediately suggests strong parallels with Ōgai's own attitudes at this time in his life: a love of travel and the arts, a sense of duty opposing freedom of the soul, and a chastened and complex attitude toward that duty. Andersen wrote the novel after a trip to Italy that freed and enlightened him, but in Copenhagen he still faced a most uncertain future as a writer. Ōgai's German experiences had much the same effect on him. It is little wonder he felt tremendously drawn to the book, although more for its tonality than for its plot.

In the Andersen novel, Federigo, a Danish friend of the

poet, gives an impassioned statement of what Italy has meant to him.

"What longings I had in my home?" said he; "they are happier who have never seen Paradise, than they who, having seen it, are driven forth, never to return. My home is beautiful; Denmark is a flowery garden, which can measure itself with any thing on the other side of the Alps; it has beech-woods and the sea. But what is earthly beauty compared with heavenly? Italy is the land of imagination and beauty; doubly happy are they who salute it for the second time!"[3]

The poet himself states that "with the soul of a child I gave myself to the rich magnificence around me, and Federigo was as happy as myself." Yet the poet soon finds himself weighed down by his gradual knowledge that human affection is never pure. Pleased by a sympathetic reaction to an account of his troubles he gave to a lady, Federigo cautions him that

. . . every heart has, in its archives, such painful memoirs. Perhaps it was her own youth's history which she heard in yours; I can believe it, for people seldom have tears for others' troubles, except when they resemble their own. We are all egotists, even in our greatest sufferings and anxieties.[4]

This theme, suggested in Ōgai's early writings, becomes a major concern in his mature works.

Toward the end of Andersen's novel, the poet's own confession resembles Ōgai's attitudes about himself at the time.

I was considered an excellent young man of talent, out of whom something might be made; and therefore, everyone took upon himself my education. My dependence permitted it to those with whom I stood connected; my good nature permitted it to all the rest. Livingly and deeply did I feel the bitterness

of my position, and yet I endured it. That was an education.
. . . no beast is, however, so cruel as man: Had I been rich and
independent, the colours of everything would have changed.
Every one of them was more prudent, more deeply grounded,
and more rational than I. I learned to smile obligingly where
I could have wept; bowed to those whom I lightly esteemed,
and listened attentively to the gossip of fools. Dissimulation,
bitterness and *ennui* were the fruits of the education which
circumstances and men afforded me. Was there then nothing
at all intellectual, no good points in me? It was I myself who
must seek for these, who must make these availing. People
riveted my thoughts upon my own individual self, and then
upbraided me for thinking too much of myself.[5]

The poet speaks here with irony and detachment, in the
fullness of his melancholy knowledge. If Andersen's novel
has a specific message, it is probably this phrase that he
puts in the mouth of Federigo: "That which is best for us
always happens; that I have found more than once, although
not in the most agreeable way." Many of Ōgai's later works
suggest a similar theme. At this time in his career, Ōgai
seemed to feel only the damage that the loss of freedom
can bring, and the statements made by Toyotarō in "The
Girl Who Danced," quoted above, are close in spirit with
those made by Andersen's poet when he says:

I was also very weak. I had vanity enough, but no pride.
That was occasioned, certainly, by my low birth, by my early
bringing up, by my dependence, and the unfortunate relationship of benefits received, in which I was placed to those around
me. The thought was ever recurring in my mind how much I
was indebted to my circumstances, and that thought bound my
tongue to the resolves of my pride. It was assuredly noble; but,
at the same time, it was weakness.[6]

Ōgai's attraction to *The Improvisatore* and the scrupu-
lous care he took in translating it, suggest that the novel
can help explicate the concerns he tried to express in his

early stories. In fact, the recreation of the novel in Japanese
occupied Ōgai's creative talents almost completely; with
the exception of the slight story in the manner of Saikaku,
"Cloth of Many Colors," written in 1897, he composed nothing more until his demon was delivered up and the translation of Andersen finished. This is not to suggest that
Ōgai had no other artistic concerns at the time; in fact,
his work on European poetry and German aesthetics put
him in the front ranks of the Japanese literary world. But
his private muse fled from him, or at least concealed herself in Andersen's pages. Ōgai did not touch on themes
related to his own experience until the composition of his
story "Hannichi" (Half a Day) in 1909, almost twenty years
after he wrote "The Girl Who Danced."

III *Poetry Translations*

Although Ōgai wrote poetry, he never considered himself
a poet in the modern (and perhaps romanticized) sense of
the word. Despite his innovative contributions to the development of a modern style of verse composition in Japan,
Ōgai's attitude toward composing poetry, viewed from the
scope of the totality of his creative work, seems closer
to that of the Tokugawa gentlemen-poets who wrote (often
in Chinese) as a cultivated pastime and an aid to self-
reflection, rather than as a devouring spiritual necessity.
Perhaps such an attitude, which lent a certain objectivity
to Ōgai's experiments, permitted him to try more styles and
a wider subject matter than might otherwise have been
possible. To begin with, Ōgai's knowledge of Western
poetry was greater than that of most of his contemporaries.
The reason for the success of the collaborative collection
Vestiges, published in 1889, was due in large measure to
his role in choosing the material. Earlier collections aimed
no higher than Longfellow and "The Charge of the Light
Brigade"; Ōgai provided the public with their first glimpses

of Goethe, Shakespeare, Kerner, and Heine, among others. According to contemporary accounts, Ōgai read the texts of all the poems aloud in both languages, then either wrote down his own translations or helped his colleagues to complete their own. German, incidentally, was the medium involved. Shakespeare was rendered into Japanese from the Schlegel translations and Byron from Heine's German versions. The German romantic vision, which in some ways resembled the Japanese view of nature expounded in *waka* and *haiku*, had a profound effect on the literary sensibility of the time, and Mignon and Ophelia began their important literary careers in Japan with the publication of this volume.

Vestiges helped suggest a wider range of emotion, subject matter, and tone possible in Western poetry; yet the translations themselves were fairly conservative in their use of the Japanese language. The poets went to the elegant diction of traditional prose and poetry. To a modern reader, the texts may sound almost as archaic (and as beautiful) as Shakespeare's English does to us.

> izure o kimi ga koibito to
> wakite shiru beki subeya aru
> kai no kamuri to tsuku tsue to
> hakeru kutsu to zo shirushi naru
>
> kara wa shinikeri waga hime to
> kare wa yomiji e tachinikeri
> kashira no kata no koke o miyo
> ashi no kata ni wa ishi tateri
>
> hitsugi o ōu kinu no iro wa
> takane no yūki to mimagainu
> namida yadoseru hana no wa wa
> nuretaru mama ni hōmurinu[7]
>
> How should I your true love know
>   from another one?

By his Cockle hat and staffe,
and his Sandal shoone.

He is dead and gone Lady,
he is dead and gone.
At his head a grasse-greene Turfe,
at his heeles a stone.

White his Shrow'd as the Mountaine Snow.
larded with sweet flowers;
Which bewept to the graue did go
with true-loue flowers.

The language of these poetry translations was close to that Ōgai used in his three German stories. Ōgai's use of what seems like traditional diction, however, is less a reflection of a conservative attitude on his part than an indication that, in 1889, there was as yet no established modern poetic language. The first work of modern literary criticism in Japan, *Shōsetsu shinzui* (The Essence of the Novel), was written only four years before, in 1885, by Tsubouchi Shōyō, who became at twenty-four the leader in a movement toward a literature of contemporary language and psychology. Shōyō took most of his ideas about Western literature from British examples he knew. By the time Ōgai returned from Germany, Shōyō had produced (in addition to his critical writing) his own novels plus translations of Scott's *Lady of the Lake*, Shakespeare's *Julius Caesar*, and parts of Edward Bulwer-Lytton's *Rienzi*. Ōgai, whose own reading had led him to make a close study of German aesthetic theory, found himself in disagreement with many of Shōyō's suppositions. The two young writers carried on a literary debate on paper that lasted two years.

Ōgai's side of the argument involved a presentation of his understanding of the ideas of Eduard von Hartmann (1842–1906), whose influential writings, especially his *Philosophy of the Unconscious*, were much admired in

Europe at the time. Shōyō used somewhat less pretentious English theories. The debate is a difficult one to follow, as the reader is confronted with Shōyō's somewhat imprecise language and Ōgai's insistence on debating fine points concerning German romanticism that were completely unfamiliar to his opponent. Briefly, Shōyō set out to indicate that literature should be based on direct experience and observation; Ōgai agreed with Shōyō that a great work of art must deal with the specific ("an image of the small world") but insisted with Hartmann that behind the specific must lie some Absolute Beauty that can invest the particular with a higher truth. Ōgai's view is perhaps abreast of its time in European terms but not exceptional. Nevertheless, between them Ōgai and Shōyō raised the level of literary criticism in Japan to a new level of seriousness.

Ōgai was as well aware of contemporary trends in European fiction as in poetry, and he showed an early interest in the work of the French author Émile Zola (1849–1902). Whatever Ōgai's allegiances to German romanticism, he could not help, perhaps on the basis of his own scientific training, but be attracted to Zola's passion for accuracy and his conviction that life could be described in literature as it was really lived. Toward the end of Ōgai's debate with Shōyō, he wrote an article on the "submerged idealism of Zola," in which he examined Zola's use of Truth instead of Beauty in searching out subjects and the means of treating them in his fiction. Despite Zola's ruthless removal of all artifice and all romanticism in art, Ōgai observed, the French writer shows himself an idealist of a deeper sort. Ōgai's early attitudes toward Zola were cautious, but the influence on his own work was important, as Ōgai was to note toward the end of his career.

The debates ended in 1892. Ōgai's subsequent activities in army medical circles and his transfer to Kokura during the "years of isolation" produced only silence. Ōgai was now forty. He had written a small number of literary works, many of them derivative from European models. Was Ōgai indeed dead, as he wrote in his Kokura statement? When he returned to Tokyo in 1902, the future of his literary career seemed uncertain. Yet in that same statement he had promised to continue writing, and so he did, in a number of new directions.

CHAPTER 3

Experiments Toward a Modern Literature
Drama and Poetry, 1902–1911

I Drama

ŌGAI'S reading of modern European literature while living in Kokura exposed him to works that were in many ways far closer to his own temperament than the writings of the German romantics he had encountered in Germany, for Ōgai's scientific training had given him a very different, and a much more modern, cast of mind; then too, the society around him was also beginning to show the complexities and confusions faced by the Europeans during their own period of urbanization. When Ōgai arrived back in Tokyo in 1902, he found that others, too, had discovered new sources of inspiration, and the figure that all were drawn to was Henrik Ibsen. In particular Tsubouchi Shōyō, Ōgai's sparring partner a decade before, had taken a strong interest in Ibsen as a model for improving the Japanese theater, and a number of translations of Ibsen's plays were being prepared. Ōgai's own first enthusiasm led him to produce a partial translation of *Brand* in 1903, and the example of Ibsen led him to try to compose for the theater himself.

Shōyō had shown the Japanese through his work on Shakespeare and Ibsen that effective drama could also be great literature. To the Meiji intelligentsia, Kabuki, the Japanese popular theater (which, at this time at least,

57

leaned toward the grotesque and colorful) seemed to have no value either as literature or as examples of human psychology. Shōyō was nevertheless convinced that the best means to create a truly contemporary theater was to add a psychological dimension to the Kabuki form, which, despite its old-fashioned pictorial qualities, continued to please a large public. Ōgai agreed, and he wrote several short plays with the idea of improving the literary quality of the drama then being presented in Tokyo.

Ōgai's first play, *Tama kushige futari Urashima* (The Jeweled Casket and the Two Urashimas), dealt with the Japanese legend of a man who lives under the sea as a kind of oriental Rip Van Winkle; Ōgai's second drama, written a year later in 1903, was a kind of lyric poem named for a young warrior, *Chōsokabe Nobuchika*, who died at the time of Hideyoshi. The play was written in an elaborate style for traditional musical performance. The third of his experimental dramas, *Nichiren Shōnin tsuji seppo* (The Street Sermon of Nichiren), was also composed in a style suitable for Kabuki production, but was an attempt to provide a psychologically acute sketch of Nichiren (1222–1282), a fanatic religious leader and patriot well known in Japanese history. Although these plays were short and somewhat tentative exercises, Ōgai showed great promise as a dramatist. At the time he wrote these plays, there were no companies for performing modern drama in Tokyo. *The Two Urashimas* was given a number of performances in 1903 by a company led by Ii Sōhō, an actor who had studied in Germany, where he had become interested in contemporary theater, and who began to introduce modern works through performances by his company. *Nichiren* was produced at the Kabukiza, the major theater for the traditional drama in Tokyo.

Ōgai ceased these experiments when he left Tokyo because of his medical duties in the Russo-Japanese war. Preoccupied with his activities there, and with a number of other literary projects after his return from the front, Ōgai wrote no more dramas until 1909, when he continued his experiments with three short plays. *Kamen* (Masks), Ōgai's only drama with a modern setting, deals with a student who has tuberculosis and discovers the meaning of life through discussions with his doctor. Their conversations are larded with fashionable references to Nietzsche. *Purumula* is the name of an Indian princess held captive in Arabia and bears a certain resemblance to Oscar Wilde's *Salome,* which Ōgai translated the same year.

Shizuka, the third of them, is probably the most satisfying of all his plays to a modern reader. Given the fact that the play is a historical drama, Ōgai has gone to considerable lengths to create the psychological dimensions of the characters, and his dialogue is rich, flexible, and colloquial, in a modern idiom far removed from the elaborate language of Kabuki. The theme of the play is one of resignation, and the attitudes expressed in *Shizuka* are close to those in his essay of the same year, "My Point of View," mentioned in chapter 1. Both texts suggest a sense of loss and gentle irony; indeed, one helps explain the other.

Shizuka, a dancer and the favorite consort of Japan's traditional romantic hero, the dashing young general Minamoto Yoshitsune (1159–1189), is a familiar character in the traditional Nō and Kabuki theater. Ōgai's variation on this traditional theme is in some ways a striking contrast to the earlier versions. Ōgai evidently took his basic information from the *Gikeiki,* a well-known medieval chronicle of Yoshitsune's life and tragic death, in which there is a lengthy and dramatic description of the murder of Shizuka's infant carried out by Adachi Kiyotsune, a retainer of Yoshitsune's jealous brother, Minamoto Yoritomo. In the original account, Yoritomo continues to hound Shizuka even after the death of Yoshitsune's child until she eventually retires from society to become a nun. Ōgai, however, selects two brief incidents from this longer account for his play.

In the first scene, some fishermen who are talking on the beach are interrupted by the arrival of Adachi and his men, who have stolen the child. Adachi gets into a boat with the child; as he does so, a character named the Mysterious Fisherman cries out:

Strike! If the left hand is in the way, cut it off. Its strength will flow into the right. Guard your right hand. It is best to guard the fingers of your right hand. I will not begrudge my left hand, nor its fingers. Listen to what I say. I do not begrudge my right hand. Nor its fingers. Kil!!¹

With these mysterious pronouncements, the scene ends.

The second scene, which takes place two months later, opens with a brief and ironic conversation between Shizuka, now bereft of child and lover, and her mother. If the first scene resembles Kabuki in the violence of its rhetoric, the second is closer to the world of Wilde and Maeterlinck, and the use of such devices as the Mysterious Fisherman in the first scene, or the Mysterious Girl in the second, may derive from such sources.

The second scene opens with the chatter of Shizuka's women attendants, soon stilled by the arrival of Adachi, who has come to see Shizuka off on her journey. He tries to convince Shizuka's mother, the nun Iso no Zenji, of his regard for them; after all, he insists, his terrible act was performed under orders.

Shizuka herself suddenly enters. "As she and Adachi exchange glances," Ōgai writes in his stage directions, "her attitude is one of resignation, manifested in a delicate irony." Adachi, seasoned enough to catch her mood, tries to make his own position clear; indeed, he tells Shizuka, he even thought of becoming a monk himself in remorse for what he did.

ADACHI: But a monk's life must be dreary beyond expectation. That priest Saigyō, who was summoned here for an

audience recently, can find himself moved by moon-
light and flowers and can write verse about it, or so
they say. But then he's a poet, and can put all his
energies into what he does. If that is the case, why
fine . . . Yet ahead of any world you abandon lies
still another. Whatever mundane things you flee,
there are more ahead. Don't you agree? It is all
very tiresome.[2]

Shizuka expresses some surprise that he is capable of
showing human feeling, then goes on to describe herself.

SHIZUKA: If you think that I am a woman who thinks only of
herself and does not consider others, you are mis-
taken. If I speak about myself in the same way that
you did, then what can I say of my own destiny? I
have been separated from the person I hold dearest.
[She pauses in melancholy reflection.] It is by no
means clear that he even remains in this world. Yet
I must go on living my shameless life. I was brought
here, made to put on my makeup, my costumes; I
sang and danced. Then I heard that if my child were
a girl, she would be helped; if a boy, he would be
killed. Yet I brazenly live on. I do not even do away
with myself. Nor do I become a nun. How easy to
criticize others for having no humane thoughts. But
first of all, I must criticize myself. Don't you agree?[3]

Shizuka's here unresolved desire for withdrawal touches
on a central concern in Ōgai's work stretching back to the
character of Ida in "The Courier," written twenty years
before. Both women are presented as artists. Ida's art is in
her music, Shizuka's in her dancing. Both eventually accept
a new set of duties, at least in part, as a means to flee their
old ones.

Toward the end of the scene, Shizuka dances and sings
a song, the text of which is traditionally said to have been
composed by the historical Shizuka herself.

> How I long for him—
> The person who vanished,
> Cleaving a way
> Through the white snows
> Of Yoshino's peaks.[4]

As the song ends, the Mysterious Girl picks up the theme of the text, Shizuka's yearning for Yoshitsune, and continues: "His traces have not yet disappeared. Before they do, you must go and seek them out. For at some point they will vanish, vanish utterly."[5] Shizuka leaves as the curtain falls.

In the chronicles, Shizuka becomes a nun. Ōgai prefers to show her at a moment in her growing awareness of her fate rather than to portray any final resolution. In the same way, Ōgai has the heroine of his last play, the 1910 *Ikutagawa* (The Ikuta River), written for production by Osanai's company, leave the stage, presumably to commit suicide, but the scene is not shown on the stage. Some Japanese critics have taken Ōgai to task for his "undramatic" structures, but in fact in his refusal to choose easy dramatic effects he was far head of his time. Ōgai's dramas, although they shed considerable light on his psychological and artistic preoccupations at the time, are too slight, too much a part of the uncertain theatrical milieu of their times to transcend them completely. Nevertheless Ōgai's dramatic work at its best leaves the reader with a sense of regret that, after a decade of increasingly successful experimentation, he turned to the translation of Western drama for stage production (often by Osanai's troupe) rather than continuing to compose for the stage himself.

II *Poetry*

Ōgai's early translations for *Vestiges* were literary and cultural experiments; the composition of original poetry became the vehicle for the expression of his deepest emotions on only a few occasions. His major collection, *Uta nikki* (The Poetry Journal), composed between 1902 and 1905, does contain some highly personal expressions of his emotional state, and hidden reflections are mirrored there of the difficult early days of his second marriage and of his participation at the front in the Russo-Japanese War of 1904–1905.

The Poetry Journal has not been a popular work of Ōgai and has been relatively little discussed among Japanese critics. Nevertheless there is much of interest in it. The collection was published in 1907 and purports to contain poems written during his military service. This is surely the case with the poems in the long first section (well over half the collection). The majority of them are dated and deal with particular events Ōgai witnessed or places he visited. Most of these are public poems in the sense that they extoll the bravery and spirit of self-sacrifice of the soldiers, even though Ōgai often decries the horrors of war. Many were published independently before the collection appeared. A very popular poem, "The Button," will illustrate the general tone of the more personal poems.

> On the day of the fighting at South Mountain
> A gold button on my sleeve
> Came loose.
> I mourn that button.
>
> On the great streets of Berlin,
> In the lanes where street lamps burned brightly,
> I bought it in a shop
> Twenty years ago.
>
> Epaulettes shining, friends
> Gold hair, a swaying girl
> They have already grown old
> Some have died.
>
> Twenty years ago a turning point in my life
> Knowing joy knowing sorrow

Buttons on my sleeve!
One of you is missing.

Broken by the warrior's bullet
Are thousands of men. I mourn them
And my button too,
This button I kept so close to me.[6]

The poem is a personal statement combining typical themes expected on such an occasion: some introspection, a certain sense of bravery, and an inevitable sense of the passing of time that has always been an important part of the Japanese poetic stance. It remains an occasional piece, even if the occasion was of some importance.

Some of the longer war poems are narrative and descriptive and often rise to considerable heights of eloquence. One for example, entitled "General Nogi," chronicles the actions of the old warrior, the great hero of the war, who led the attack on Port Arthur, when he learned of the death of his two sons in battle. The image Ōgai presents of the general, looking into the faces of his men under the glittering winter stars, is effective because it seems the product of emotions really felt by the poet. The poem, incidentally, marks Ōgai's first literary interest in Nogi, who figures later as the inspiration for some of Ōgai's historical accounts of ritual suicide.

The Poetry Journal, however, contains four other short sections. The first of them contains Ōgai's translations of such nineteenth-century German poets as Nicholas Lenau, August von Platen, Karl Bleibtreu, D. F. Liliencron, and Eduard Mörike. This exercise in translation seems to have served as a stylistic notebook for Ōgai, through which he examined themes and techniques used by German poets in composing their own war poetry. In making the translations, Ōgai employed a style of composition he also used in writing his own poems in that volume, a style marked by the introduction of modern vocabulary into what was basically a conservative poetic diction.

The latter three sections, all rather short, present some of the most obscure texts Ōgai composed. There are war scenes among them, but many have to do with his emotional relationships with his family and others. The section "Dreams" is particularly complex and obscure. Here, for example, is a poem entitled "Flower Garden."

> The blooming flowers   poinsettias
> Thick colors
> The flesh of the leaves   glossy
> Refulgent
> The master of the garden   who might it be
>
> The flowers bloom, yet   ordinary
> Flowers they must not be
> The leaves grow thick, yet   ordinary
> Leaves they cannot be
> In the master is some magic strength
>
> Blooming flowers   become the red blood
> Of my countenance
> Refulgent leaves   become my flesh:
> So be it! Conceal it from the world.
>
> Flowers in the darkness   disgorging poison
> Frightening visions   night after night
> Coming out of the leaves   snakes swarming
> The very bed chastises:
> So be it! Conceal it from the world.[7]

The references here seem most ambiguous. Is the garden a garden of sin? If Ōgai is the suffering *persona* presented here, what are the meanings of the symbols? To whom is the poem directed? Some critics have tentatively suggested that a certain number of these poems were composed as early as 1902, and that Ōgai either revised them during his military service or merely included them in the volume. They are written in a style utterly different from that of the "public" poetry concerning the war and seem to speak in a private language of symbols ultimately understood only by their author. As poems they may lack the final mastery of form and technique that would have led to a more general recognition of their worth; yet one is as close to the man in these dozen pages as in any of his works.

One reason for the relative lack of attention *The Poetry Journal* has received in terms of the development of modern poetry may stem from the fact that Ōgai's diction hesitates and wavers between the old forms of poetic statement and the new ones he and others had developed elsewhere. When Ōgai set out for the front he was given as farewell gifts two collections of poetry: an edition of the ninth-century *Manyōshū*, the oldest collection of Japanese poetry, given him by the *waka* poet Sasaki Nobutsuna, and a collection of translations of French symbolist poetry by the translator, Ueda Bin. Ōgai seems to look in both directions for inspiration and the differences in style are too great to be easily reconciled. When Ōgai returned from the war, however, he continued his experiments in the newer styles. These later efforts were published in 1915 in a second volume, *Sara no ki* (The Sal Tree). Here Ōgai divided the collection into three distinct categories: translations, poems entirely in the modern vernacular, and a section of traditional *waka*. The sharp separation of styles produced his best work.

Included among the translations are works of the contemporary German poets Richard Dehmel, Christian Morgenstern, and the Viennese poet Klabund (Alfred Henschke), perhaps best remembered for his German adaptation of a Chinese Yüan drama, *The Circle of Chalk*, made from an earlier French translation, that eventually inspired Brecht's *Caucasian Chalk Circle*. These writers were important figures in German poetry at this time, and

Ōgai's translations of their work, along with his work on Rilke, had a profound effect on the later development of modern Japanese poetry; indeed Ōgai and others made available in Japanese more modern German poetry than was available in English at the time. Ōgai's diction here as well was in a thoroughly contemporary idiom, and the traces of traditional Japanese poetic usage that gave a slightly romantic air to the translations in *Vestiges* and *The Poetry Journal* disappeared almost completely. Among the translations included in the volume is a charming curiosity, a translation into elegant and simple Japanese of the libretto of Gluck's opera, *Orpheus and Euridice,* commissioned for a Japanese production of the opera. Ōgai's memories of a performance of the opera he saw in Germany and his discussion of the difficulties of matching words to music show a considerable lyric sensitivity.

Ōgai's own fifteen-odd poems in the modern style show a complete amalgamation of the contemporary language. In many ways these poems, modest in emotional scope though they may be, are among the first successful poems in modern Japanese. The images he employs are simple but perhaps striking enough to survive in translation.

Fire

An invisible broom moves:
The night wind sweeps askance
The macadam street at the crossing.

Shops glow with electric lights, yet
As I walk away without a glance,
A flutter of newspaper, thrown away,
Touches my shoetips.

Bells break out. Paper lanterns hurry by.
Shadows run. The rapid metal voices
Crowd my ears.

The earth roars. People, in great confusion
Rush in every direction. Roaring, rumbling:
The stark red engine pumps.[8]

The third section of the book contains one hundred *waka*,
the traditional thirty-one-syllable verse form. Ōgai's interest in *waka* was of long standing, and by 1907 he had
gathered together a number of important poets from several existing groups to work together on an informal basis
to achieve a transformation of the somewhat old-fashioned
waka style into a form more flexible and responsive to
modern life. In the course of those meetings, Ōgai wrote
a certain number of poems himself, some of which were
published in poetry magazines. Ōgai wrote in his preface
to *The Sal Tree* that he did not intend those poems for
publication and finally permitted them to appear in collected form only at the repeated urgings of his friends.
Ōgai was not really a master of the form, and his reticence
is understandable; nevertheless he did contribute to the
development of the modern *waka*. He introduced vocabulary never before considered possible in *waka* poetry, including foreign words: no other poet of the time would
have used the words "piano," "Richard Wagner," "absinthe,"
"Olympus," or "Nazareth" in traditional poetry. Many
poems are merely pleasant little sketches, but some seem
more revealing, such as:

> nani hitotsu
> yoku wa mizariki
> sei o fumu
> waga ashi amari
> sukoyaka nareba
>
> Not one thing
> Have I seen fully:
> As I walk life's road
> My feet are too vigorous.[9]

Ōgai's experiments as a poet, like his work as a dramatist, had considerable historical importance in the development of modern Japanese literature, and his efforts to master those forms helped him to develop a more flexible and evocative writing style. If his accomplishments were not always of the highest caliber, the experience of writing verse and dialogue nevertheless provided Ōgai with a second apprenticeship that led to the composition of his much greater prose works of the period.

CHAPTER 4

Man in His Society, 1909-1912

THE efforts expended by Ōgai and others to provide a conceptual and linguistic means for the composition of modern poetry and drama were not necessary for prose fiction. Ōgai's own contributions and those of other writers had produced by the turn of the century a supple and effective modern vernacular written language. Ōgai now took that language and, in an extraordinary burst of creative activity from his forty-ninth to his fifty-second year, produced a series of works that marked his first period of maturity as a writer. His apprenticeship had been a long one; now, the results were astounding. The enormous quantity of works produced during this brief time can be roughly divided into three categories: short stories, novels, and philosophical dialogues. Each type of literary creation filled a different but related function in the totality of his work.

The short stories, well over a dozen in number, veer in and out of autobiography; they often seem to represent Ōgai's first reactions as an artist to his situation as a man. Even the slightest of the stories are successful to some degree since Ōgai manages to maintain a sufficient aesthetic distance from his subject matter; indeed, the more he can do this, the more effective the stories seem. As a whole these stories might be classified as informal studies, sketches for the emotional elements, and sometimes the intellectual elements, developed in the four novels written during the same period.

In his short sketch, "Tsuina" (Exorcising Demons), Ōgai

wrote of Balzac waking to write at night and considered the nature of his own "night thoughts."

How and what to write? I am exhausted when I return home from the government office. People usually have a drink at dinner and then cheerfully go to sleep until the next morning. But I turn the lamp low and sleep for just a while, with the resolution of getting up shortly. At midnight I wake up. My mind is a little recovered. I stay up from then until two o'clock and write.

Thoughts of the day are different from those of the night. It often happens that during the night I believe I have satisfactorily solved a problem I couldn't solve during the day, but when I reappraise this the next morning, it frequently turns out to be no solution at all. There is something unreliable about the thoughts of the night.[1]

"Unreliable," highly personal, these dozen short works serve as probes, sent out in various directions, seeking the means to resolve and transcend the contradictions Ōgai felt in every aspect of his personal life and in the life of his times. The stories are much better understood when juxtaposed with each other than read in isolation. Ōgai often continued to treat a similar problem in several stories from different points of view.

The question of style was also an important consideration for Ōgai; he had ideas he wished to express, ideas seldom expressed in Japanese literature before. "Isn't it a very shackled notion," he wrote in "Exorcising Demons," "to insist that one should write literary prose about certain things in a certain way? I, with my 'thoughts in the night,' have concluded that what we call literary prose may be written about anything, and in any style."[2]

In none of the works of this period did Ōgai set out to "write a story," but to express an idea in narrative terms. The distinction, so important to him, requires that the reader first grasp the central import of a given work, then go back to see how the details have been placed together to produce the effect desired. Little is wasted. Even when such an economy of means seems barren on first perusal, a further examination invariably reveals an exquisite artistic restraint and discrimination.

Ōgai's knowledge of Europe, his early experiences in Germany, strengthened by his work on translations of fiction, drama, poetry, and philosophy, gave him a strong and ironic sense of the discrepancy between the contemporary reality of a Japan copying a still badly understood Western model and a Japan potentially capable of creating and sustaining a healthy culture. Even the settings of the stories can create a palpable atmosphere that expresses Ōgai's moral concern. In his 1910 story "Under Reconstruction," the ill-assorted mixture of East and West in a gaudy western-style hotel serves to draw the scorn of the protagonist.

The water in the canal appeared completely stationary. On the other side he could see a row of wooden buildings. They looked like houses of assignation. Except for a woman with a child on her back, walking slowly back and forth outside one of the houses, there was no one in sight. At the far right, the massive red-brick structure of the Naval Museum imposingly blocked his view.

Watanabe sat down on the sofa and examined the room. The walls were decorated with an ill-assorted collection of pictures: nightingales on a plum tree, an illustration from a fairy tale, a hawk. The scrolls were small and narrow, and on the high walls they looked strangely short, as if the bottom portions had been tucked under and concealed. Over the door was a large framed Buddhist text. And this is meant to be the land of art, thought Watanabe.[3]

This short passage (from a fine translation by Ivan Morris) shows something of the spare power of Ōgai's mature language. The sentences are short. The words chosen are simple and specific. The observations, all visual, are precisely stated. Only in the final sentence is the reader given the protagonist's own response to what he has seen; and by the time the last sentence is reached, the reader is able to concur with that judgment. Clarity produces the effect desired.

The same view is described from an (evidently) nearby Japanese restaurant in "Exorcising Demons." The atmosphere here is intended to be a somewhat more wholesome one.

All around me it was hushed. The sound of the rain clogs rose from the street by the moat. Built into the high and massive sliding doors by which I sat, at about the height of my elbow, there were two small movable panels. I opened one and looked out, but there was no one to be seen. . . . Everything had become grey; even the gaudy new Naval Memorial Museum appeared as if brushed over with grey. A solitary auto with no rider but the driver came from the direction of the Naval School and slowly made its way west.

I closed the panel. The lights came on. I smoked my cigar and looked around the room. In this large, airy, attractive room, I thought, nothing impedes the eye. There are no disagreeable hangings on the wall. Despite the inclusion of that inevitable relic, the *tokonoma*, the *kakemono* and flower arrangements are hardly conspicuous. It is a most suitable place to sit and eat delectable things and watch the geisha perform. One might say that this is Japan's architecture, in these materialistic times.[4]

Ōgai is searching for the quality of life to transcend the divisiveness of the time, and this quest becomes the major theme of his later writings. The possibility of harmony between idea, human character, and social situation became the central virtue Ōgai sought. He found little harmony manifested in the Japan of 1910. One means to transcend was to withdraw, a theme that had occupied Ōgai off and on since his early story "The Courier." The tension between participation and withdrawal underlies

many of the strories in this period as well; and the treatment was often highly personal.

Marriage and celibacy are often contrasted. In "Doku-
shin" (Living Alone, 1910), Ōgai suggests the peace and
calm that comes from isolation. The story is based on his
Kokura experience, and his description of the changing
seasons he suggests a calm contemplation and a close
observation reminiscent of the values of traditional Japanese literature. The love and care shown by the protagonist
to his friends, drinking together on a Sunday night, bespeak
an almost Confucian calm.

> The master, who led an extremely simple bachelor's life, sent
> his maid Také out to buy noodles, boiled them in the kitchen,
> and served saké to his friends. And when he served tea at
> home, he would send out for baked sweet potatoes, saying
> they were better than a well-known kind of cake called *tsuru
> no ko*. At the Toppan bridge crossroad, where the corner turns
> at Kyō-machi, there is an old man with a towel wrapped around
> his head who sets up a kettle, calling out, "Piping hot! Just
> right!" and sells potatoes there. Although the master did not
> drink himself, when he provided hospitality for friends to whom
> he felt close, he always sent for those favorite noodles. They
> came from a shop two or three doors down from where the man
> with the kettle sat, where the faded, dark blue curtain hung,
> dyed with the name *bunroku*.
> The master shared only in the noodles, and with a happy
> smile on his normally indifferent face, he watched his two
> friends as they drank.[5]

The genial banter of the protagonist and his guests
eventually breaks off as they urge him to marry, and
various examples of the state, good and bad, are produced
as evidence. At the end of the evening, alone with himself,
he realizes that at forty, and long since divorced, he
perhaps feels no more desire for the opposite sex. His
final thoughts before retiring alternate between the memory
of desire (a country girl he once saw at a funeral) and the

problem of how to respond to the repeated urgings of his mother to remarry.

The state of life sketched here, retiring, gentle, seems in sharp contrast to the atmosphere created in "Hannichi" (Half a Day), written a year earlier in 1909. Here the protagonist is married, and the conflicts between himself, his wife, and his mother threaten to destroy him altogether, and he is forced to retreat into silence. His wife, willful and lacking in self-discipline, cannot bear this attitude.

At times like this his silence made her furious. She would close in on him with "Say something!" her long, white fingers clutching at his wrist. Then she would declare war and threaten to cut off her hair or to cut her throat. Sometimes she would make her usual threat to take Tama and go away. And there were other times of fragile reconciliation just because they had touched. Now, because it was the aftermath of one explosion early in the morning, she did not even try to fight. It would be too difficult for her to introduce the problem of "going somewhere" a second time. Considering the time of day it was, and as things were different from the first couple of years of their marriage, she could no longer expect even those fragile reconciliations. As was to be expected, she remained silent. The room was hushed once more. Now and then the ticking of the clock could be heard.[6]

Eventually the protagonist is forced to speculate as to whether or not his wife might be somehow deranged, a "borderline case." In "Hebi" (The Snake), written in 1911, Ōgai continues the theme of domestic conflict; again the elements in tension are between a mother, her weak-willed son (this time a wealthy provincial artistocrat) and his wife who, like her predecessor in "Half a Day," is cruel to her mother-in-law to the point where the old woman dies, dejectedly, in silence. Later the wife, going to a Buddhist altar set up for her dead mother-in-law, sees a large snake inside and seemingly becomes deranged.

These stories reveal something of Ōgai's personal difficulties with his second wife, but they are more important than their materials, and they seem to represent artistic manifestations of a personality trying to understand, and so transcend, the emotional impasse reached in an imperfect human relationship. The means to transcendence becomes a positive detachment.

In "Hanako" (1910), Ōgai wrote of the Japanese actress and dancer who posed for Rodin.[7] Kubota, the young man who takes her to meet the sculptor, finds her "no more presentable than a chambermaid." While Rodin is with her, Kubota reads a passage from an essay of Baudelaire entitled *Morale du Joujou* (A Philosophy of Toys). Ōgai paraphrases the French author as follows:

> After a child has played with a toy for a certain time, he is possessed by a desire to break it. He wonders what may be beyond the object itself. If the toy is one that moves, he wishes to search out the source of its impetus. The child thus goes from *physique* to *métaphysique*, from science to metaphysics.[8]

Ōgai chose Baudelaire to explain Rodin's grasp of the inner beauty behind Hanako's undistinguished face, and his choice of subject matter for this brief but perfect little story seems dictated by an attempt to find a means to transcend the surface contradictions and pettiness of everyday life to find the ideal that Rodin tells Kubota represents "the inner flame, that can be seen as it penetrates through the form; that alone is interesting."

Two other important stories, "Asobi" (Play, 1910) and "Hyaku Monogatari" (The Tale of a Hundred Candles, 1911) continue the investigation of withdrawal and transcendence.

"Play," written in an ironic mode, is usually taken as an important example of Ōgai's conception of a bystander to life (despite the fact that he wrote the story during perhaps the busiest year of his career); in the context of his other work, however, the story suggests a necessary means to transcend pettiness of every description. The protagonist, a minor writer and bureaucrat named Kimura, is a shrunken, half-comic version of Ōgai himself. Ōgai again chooses to write of the attitudes of a child, as he did in "Hanako," but for different purposes.

Kimura looks after things in a leisurely fashion, doing his tasks steadily one by one. At such a time he invariably has a cheerful look. Kimura's feelings at such a time are somewhat difficult to describe. As much as anything, he feels rather like a child at play. And as far as such "playing" goes, some of it is compelling, some of it is tedious. His present tasks are among those he regards as tedious. Work for his government office is, of course, nothing to joke about. He is well aware of the fact that he is merely a tiny cog in the vast government machine. In fact, it is precisely because he is aware of this situation that he can regard his own attitude with which he carried out those duties as "play." The cheerfulness of his expression is a manifestation of his attitude.[9]

Art and creation, on the other hand, are pleasant play. But the objective presence of a mind seeking something beyond remains the impetus behind the attitudes Ōgai himself holds. Kimura daydreams of war and voyages to romantic spots while stamping his documents. He is, for Ōgai at least, a partially comic figure, who cannot seek beyond the limits of his own restricted mental and social environment.

"Play" is a striking story, however, and may well have represented a stage in Ōgai's own spiritual development, a hard view of himself and his contemporary society that prepared him to move toward his final historical "Apollonian" stories from Japanese and Chinese history. "The Tale of a Hundred Candles," written the following year, is a more thoughtful, less ironic description of a man at play, so much so, in fact, that Shikamaya, the protagonist, drops out of active society almost altogether.

The story is told in the first person (presumably by Ōgai himself) and describes a party held on a riverboat during a festival to which the narrator was invited. The title of the story refers to the entertainment provided at the party. An old Edo custom is invoked: the guests assemble, light candles, and tell ghost stories. When the candles burn down, the ghost is supposed to appear. The party, however, held in a noisy and artificial atmosphere, is a failure, and the only ghost may be the host himself, who feels removed from any meaningful contact with his own guests. The narrator, watching the scene in his own detachment, observes the host and the woman with him, who "seemed like a nurse to a sick patient." He reflects on the nature of those who seem by their character to remain onlookers in the world.

I have thought often, and deeply, about those born to be bystanders. I myself have no incurable disease. Yet I, too, am inherently a bystander. From the time I first began to play with other children, and even when I grew to adulthood and made my way in the world, and with every kind of person in society, I have never been able to throw myself into the whirlpool and enjoy myself to the depths of my being, no matter what kind of excitement may have been stirred in me. Even though I have made my appearance on the stage of human activity, I have never played a role worthy of the name. The most I have achieved has been the position of a supernumerary. And indeed I have felt most like myself when I had no need to mount that stage and, like a fish in water, could remain at ease among the bystanders. With these feelings, I watched Shikamaya, and as I did so, I realized that I felt as though I had met an old friend in a foreign country. I felt as though one bystander had discovered another.[10]

The narrator then goes on to speculate as to what may have caused this man, despite his attitude of retiring from life, to give such a party. He concludes that Shikamaya may have "the same attitude as a writer, who at the same time he creates may look dispassionately with the eye of a critic at his own work."

Ōgai's use of a narrator in "The Tale of a Hundred Candles" is an effective device to objectify his narrative. In his early stories his use of an observer was less successful. In "The Girl Who Danced," the juxtaposition of himself, or the *persona* so much like himself, with his material was perhaps too close; in "The Courier," written only slightly later, he created a bystander who serves, admittedly a bit awkwardly, as a means to objectify the events described. In that story, the bystander is the young Japanese officer Kobayashi; in the 1910 story "Hanako," Kubota, the young Japanese medical student who brings the Japanese dancer to see Rodin, serves the same function. In "The Tale of a Hundred Candles," the balance between action and reflection is nicely struck: the narrator comes to understand himself as he observes the actions of the others.

The stories written in this three-year period found Ōgai, now nearing fifty, delving into his own human experience, personally, socially, spiritually. The stories may be fragments, but the four novels he wrote between 1909 and 1912 represent a more formal, and in some ways, a more typically "literary" attempt to grapple with the same problems. Ōgai also experimented with certain literary problems of his day, and in fact many Japanese critics analyze the novels in terms of Ōgai's presumed "antinaturalist" bias. These literary quarrels, however, have little to do with the ultimate purposes of the works in Ōgai's own mind, and no discussion of the arguments is reproduced here. Certainly for a foreign reader the value of these novels must lie in the texts themselves rather than in the literary and sociological commentaries made on them by Japanese historians.

In all four novels Ōgai took over certain aspects of his own youth as his basic material. The protagonists are all different people. They go through their own unique experiences. Yet many elements are repeated: a male protagonist from the country comes to Tokyo, makes connections with distinguished colleagues (as Ōgai did with Nishi Amane), goes through formative experiences in school and university, comes to experience relationships with women, then comes to find a certain disgust with the superficial elements in his society. Most important of all the narratives all show the relentless development in the protagonists of a tendency toward self-reflection that leads to a strong sense of objectivity about life. The four books are four paths to a goal of self-identification in the profoundest sense. Japanese critics have often taken Ōgai's personal experiences, which serve as the building blocks for his structure, and try to identify the various models Ōgai used for his characters. Fortunately the books can stand without any such exegesis; in fact, such efforts to reduce the novels to autobiography merely draw attention away from their real purposes, and their real merits.

Ōgai's themes are first adumbrated in *Vita Sexualis*, written in 1909. The publication caused a tremendous scandal and the issue of *The Pleiades* in which it appeared was banned by the government; reading it now, such a reaction seems almost quaint. There is nothing remotely pornographic about the account. *Vita Sexualis* is truly daring, however, in that Ōgai manages to examine frankly the limitations of human sexual desire. The *persona* of the novel is Kanai, a professor of Eastern and Western philosophy. Kanai is convinced that an overemphasis on sexual desire in Japanese and Western "naturalistic" fiction of the period somehow represents an abnormal preoccupation of the authors concerned; he also feels strongly the distinction between desire and love. Kanai, who regards himself as an average man in this respect, decides to write down the history of his own sexual awakening in order to understand himself. By writing such a memoir, Kanai sets out to objectify his past by recreating it. The purpose of writing such an account, he indicates, is that he can show it to his son, who will soon graduate from secondary school. Kanai hopes to guide and enlighten him.

The impressionistic sections that make up the bulk of the book are a chronicle of growing up, and they show a man in the midst of remembering and recreating in the objectivity of time a sense of how he developed an awareness of life. First, we are shown a child's experiences, then the complexities of student dormitory life. Kanai's own attitudes are compared with those of his two best friends, Koga and Kojima. Their life is remarkably innocent. In fact, the image of Kanai's romantic dreams never materialized more fully than his vague reflections on the sight of a girl he saw standing in a doorway.

. . . on the north side was a curio shop. The paper sliding screens of the shop were always half closed. Pasted in a corner of these sliding doors was a rectangular sheet of paper, and on it were the characters for "Akisada," written as if a sign painter had done them. Each time I went to Kosuge on my way there and back, I felt a joy in passing those sliding doors. And once when I saw a girl standing in the open space between the doors, I felt, for about a week, some undefinable satisfaction. When I found the girl wasn't there, I felt, for a week, a vague dissatisfaction.

Probably she wasn't much of a beauty. Her pinkish face, though, was as fresh as dew that has just emerged, her bright eyes with a charm impossible to describe. In her hair, just washed and set in the *shimada* style, was no red ribbon or ornament. During the summer she would have on a cotton kimono in a gay, lively pattern. In winter she was dressed in a kimono of common silk with a replaceable neckband. She always wore a clean apron.

From that time until long past my graduation from the university—no, that's not so—until the day I went abroad two

years after my graduation, this girl was quite definitely the
heroine of my beautiful dream.[11]

Romantic calm is possible for the young Kanai, but
boisterous vulgarity is not. He is taken at the time of his
graduation from his university to a geisha party. He
dislikes the atmosphere and resents being snubbed by a
geisha anxious to impress a professor sitting nearby.

From that very moment I felt as if I were completely awake.
I felt, for example, as if I were looking at violent waves after
I had been flung on the seashore from inside a swirling mael-
strom. All the members of the party were mirrored in my eyes
with perfect objectivity.[12]

This minor incident changes his whole mode of appre-
hension toward women. Kanai understands clearly that
the point of view expressed in his memoirs is particular
to him, observing that "... I don't believe any work of
art can escape the label 'self-vindication.' For man's life
is his attempt at vindicating himself." He goes on to
describe the traditional Japanese marriage proposals made
to him, his unwilling visit to a house of prostitution, and
his reactions to women he meets in Germany (including an
incident that resembles the opening scene of "A Record
of Froth on the Water"). All of these accounts are
presented in a spirit of a perfect, and a humane, objectivity.
Kanai concludes his narrative by remarking that "a person
without passion cannot be a good subject for autobiography" and reflects on the fact that because he has had
an excessively thorough knowledge of himself ever since
he was a boy, "that knowledge had completely blasted his
passion in its embryo."

Ōgai acknowledges here the tension between what he
later called the Dionysian and Apollonian modes of writing,
and his natural preference for the latter. Kanai states
that his "tiger of passion has been tamed," and this use

of a typical Chinese image for sexual desire suggests the traditional quietist ideals that were in keeping with Ōgai's own attitudes. Indeed, the last images in the novel are drawn from elements typical of the atmosphere in a contemplative Chinese poem and represent Ōgai's first mention of an ideal outside his own time.

> Having thought everything over in this way, Mr. Kanai slowly reread his manuscript from the beginning. And when he had read it to the end, he found the night much further advanced. The rain had stopped without his realizing it. Drops of water falling on a rock from the mouth of a water pipe fell intermittently, making a sound like the beating of the chevron-stone of ancient China.[13]

Ōgai goes on to pose one final question: can one human being understand another? Kanai speculates that even his own son might not grasp his point of view. "He couldn't tell beforehand what the effect on his son might be. If his son read it and became like him, what then? Would the boy be happy or unhappy? He couldn't tell about that either."

Ōgai's next novel, *Seinen* (Youth, 1910), reexamines many of the same themes concerned with growing into self-awareness. The protagonist, Koizumi Jun'ichi arrives in Tokyo, like his predecessor Kanai, but his quest is for a way to join the intellectual and literary world he so admires. *Youth* comes closest to showing the nature of Ōgai's own quest for artistic self-identification, and his descriptions of the intellectual life of his day makes *Youth* a priceless document in modern Japanese cultural history. Ōgai's artistic purposes push the book through a few awkward sequences to produce one of his most sustained accomplishments. It is not a perfect novel but surely represents Ōgai's most absorbing contribution among all the works written in his middle years.

The composition of the novel (the longest work of

fiction he composed) seems, on the evidence of Ōgai's comments, to have given him a certain amount of trouble. The difficulty of giving fictional flesh to discussions of ideas is one artistic problem he was not able to resolve in any fully satisfactory fashion. As a result, the long conversations between Jun'ichi and his friend Ōmura during which they stroll and discuss art, aesthetics, and the nature of life, slow and divert the main impetus of the narrative, although the discussions themselves are often fascinating. On the other hand, it can be argued that such discussions were indeed the means by which intellectuals of the period learned about Western literature and philosophy; and the enthusiastic reactions of Ōgai's young men to Ibsen, Maeterlinck, and Nietzsche were very much a part of the atmosphere he wished to convey. Among the minor characters in *Youth* are also a number of Japanese literary portraits, and by other names we are introduced to the personalities and ideas of Masamune Hakuchō, Natsume Sōseki, and others.

Jun'ichi wishes to become a writer. He is fascinated by what he takes to be intellectual life and by the play of ideas he finds in the conversations he has with his new acquaintances in Tokyo. Soon, however, he realizes that these ideas come to him from the outside and that he has lived through, and experienced, nothing. He feels himself passive, unable to create from any inner stimulus. Ōgai sketches here his version of that familiar figure of the sensitive young writer who can find nothing to write about.

Much of Jun'ichi's growing self-awareness comes through his observations of women. Oyuki, a modest and attractive girl of a relatively traditional cast of mind, does not stimulate him. An attractive geisha who gives him her card at a party sets him to thinking of the close interrelationship between vanity and real affection, but he never sees her again. Jun'ichi is searching for the kind of emancipated woman his "advanced" ideas make attractive to him. He thinks he has found her when he meets Mrs. Sakai, the widow of a famous professor of French. Appropriately enough, Jun'ichi meets her at the opening night of the first professional production in Japan of an Ibsen drama, *John Gabriel Borkman* (translated for Osanai's production by Ōgai himself, as was noted above). She has learning, sophistication, and beauty. Jun'ichi becomes obsessed with Mrs. Sakai, visits her home, borrows books from her library, and keeps up every contact he can with her. At the climax of the novel, Jun'ichi, moved by complex emotions he scarcely understands himself, follows her to Hakone, a mountain resort near Tokyo, only to find that she is there with a friend, the painter Okamura. To them, he suddenly realizes, he is only an amusing child. He returns after this last interview to his hotel in great despondency; with the noise of a raucous party in the background, he forces himself to look with great objectivity on the emotional dependence he has felt for Mrs. Sakai. His self-understanding is enough to save him.

. . . in fact, as far as Mrs. Sakai was concerned, he really had no right to feel any sense of discontent. In fact, why did he feel so dissatisfied? Certainly not over any despair at having lost her. It was no more than a wound received by his self-esteem.[14]

Some of the most effective portions of the book are those that purport to be passages from Jun'ichi's diaries, in which his reactions are presented in the most direct and forceful way. Here are a few excerpts from the first entry in the diary, presented in chapter 10.

November 30. Clear. I suppose it is foolish of me to note down the weather as if I were keeping some sort of daily record. For some reason I simply cannot sustain the effort of keeping a diary. The last time I visited Ōmura we talked about this, and he said, "Mankind is restrained by so many things;

so why should you bind and limit yourself even further?" A man lives—there is surely no reason for him to go fussily about making a diary about it. Yet the problem remains—if not bound by a diary, what to do? That is the problem. For what purpose has the self been liberated? That is the problem.

To write. To compose. To create, as God created all things. That was my first idea. But I cannot....

To be alive ... to live our life....

A response seems simple. But the contents of that response are not simple at all.

In fact, does a Japanese know what it means to live? Beginning with grade school, we think to hurry on through that period of our lives. We assume that Living is still ahead. When we leave school, we begin to work, determined to succeed. Because Living still lies ahead of us. Yet ahead there is no Living.

The present is a line divided between past and future. If Living does not exist on this line, then it exists nowhere. Thus, what am I to do with myself?[15]

Jun'ichi's search for the truth of art and for the truth in himself becomes successful, as did Kanai's, as he gains an increasingly objective sense of himself. Even at the height of his infatuation with Mrs. Sakai, he experiences the moment when he can see the reality of his own situation with great clarity. Jun'ichi visits her at home and finds her polite but preoccupied; they have an empty conversation, and he gains a new image of her. Jun'ichi describes his reaction as follows.

Her face was practically a mask. I put out feelers, half against my will, looking for some shadow of emotion; yet everything stopped in her dark-brown pupils. What might be behind them? In her face was a kind of oppressive heaviness, like a summer sky weary of good weather, expecting a thunderstorm. I might wish to describe her eyes as those of a beast of prey that has located its victim; yet there was not this ferocity to them. If there are such creatures as nymphs in the tropics, would they not have eyes like these? If not that, then perhaps her face might be described as a face in death. The complexion of a beautiful, dead person.[16]

Suddenly, he realized, they were speaking as strangers. Jun'ichi sees her for the first time as an "opponent."

At the end of the novel, freed from Mrs. Sakai, Jun'ichi now gains through his first genuine emotional experience the ability he has lacked until now: the power to create within himself. Jun'ichi decides to write of the past, a decision that mirrors Ōgai's own deepest artistic preoccupations at the time. The importance of Jun'ichi's decision extends far beyond the confines of *Youth.* Ōgai, through Jun'ichi, has identified the deepest layer of his artistic consciousness.

When Jun'ichi thought over precisely what he wished to write, he realized that what he had in his mind was something quite apart from the sort of thing that was then popular. What he had in mind was to write down a local legend told him by his grandmother when she was still alive. In fact he had made several previous attempts to write it down.... Now he decided to compose his text in contemporary language and with a contemporary subtlety of observation, so as to attempt to retain the flavor of the old story. That was his plan.[17]

Jun'ichi's decision to go to the past becomes, after 1912, the chief impetus in Ōgai's own creative writing. The scene in the novel where Jun'ichi reaches this decision is surely a reflection of Ōgai's own determination to examine not only his own personal past, which he had been doing in his stories and novels of the period, but the past of his whole rapidly changing culture.

Ōgai's next novel, *Gan* (Wild Goose), written the following year in 1911, is his first attempt at an examination of the past, although a past still linked to Ōgai's own experience. Set in Tokyo in the 1880s, early in the Meiji period, Ōgai creates an atmosphere considerably removed

from the far more westernized Japan of 1911. The novel
begins with the sentence "This is an old-fashioned story,"
and the relatively sentimental plot seems fully appropriate
to the slightly archaic atmosphere he wished to create.
The names of the characters change, and there are many
new details, but the outlines of the narrative are close
to those of the earlier books. The novel opens with a short
narration in the first person (possibly Ōgai himself)
giving certain details about the life of a fellow student
named Okada, whose walks through Tokyo took him by a
house where he saw a girl looking out at him. He begins
to feel a fondness for her. The minor incident in *Vita
Sexualis* now becomes the focal point of the later novel,
and Ōgai's interest shifts to the female character, the girl
Otama.

Otama was first married off by her parents in an unhappy
situation, then made the mistress of an unpleasant money-
lender named Suezō in order to restore the family finances.
Her fate might be that of a typical heroine in a Tokugawa
Kabuki melodrama. Ōgai, however, wishes to see beyond
the sentimental clichés in his "old-fashioned story," in order
to examine past attitudes from his contemporary point of
view, and he pictures Otama's awakening sense of self with
the same kind of precision he showed in creating the
character of Jun'ichi in *Youth*.

... one day she was startled by an awareness of something
sprouting inside her. This embryo within her imagination had
been conceived under the threshold of consciousness and, suddenly taking definite shape, had sprung out.

Her aim in life had been her father's happiness, so she had
become a mistress, almost forcibly persuading the old man to
accept. She knew she had degraded herself to the lowest limits,
yet she had still sought a kind of spiritual comfort in the un-
selfishness of her choice. But when the person who supported
her turned out to be a usurer, she did not know how to cope
with this new source of misfortune. The thought tormented her,

and she was unable to remove it. She had gone to her father to tell him about it and to ask him to share her pain. But when she had visited him and had seen him living comfortably for the first time, she didn't want to pour a drop of poison in the saké cup he held in his hand. Whatever pain the decision might cost her, she was determined to keep her sadness to herself. And when she had made this decision, the girl, who had always depended on others, had felt for the first time her own independence.

After that, she secretly began to watch what she said and did, and when Suezō came, she started to serve him self-consciously instead of accepting him frankly and sincerely as she had previously done. She would be with him in the room, but her real self was detached, watching the scene from the side.[18]

Ōgai's description of Otama's awakening seems to parallel his own experience: in thrall to his own traditionally minded society, he discovered his own intellectual and spiritual independence in Europe but continued to serve the state self-consciously, always keeping his distance. The themes of rebellion and authority, first stated in the early works, here receive a second artistic manifestation. Yet Otama is not a mere fleshing-out of an abstract idea; she is a successful character in her own right. Her motivations and her self-discovery ring true.

The awakening of Otama's sense of self, and her objective sense of her social reality first makes her lonely, then makes her daring. Okada speaks with her briefly when he helps rescue her caged bird from a snake. After this incident she decides that she will take the initiative and speak to him as he passes on his daily walk. Unfortunately the conversation never takes place, as Okada is detained in a curious incident that gives the novel its title. Okada and his friends decide to throw stones at a flock of wild geese; Okada himself hits one, and it falls dead in the pond. The young men take the goose away to cook and eat it. Okada passes Otama's house with all his friends and does not

speak to her at all. He leaves soon thereafter for study in
Germany, as did his predecessor in *Vita Sexualis.*

The atmosphere of early Meiji, and the slow sense of
social awakening of which Otama is the focus, are well
expressed in the prose style of the novel. Ōgai takes considerable care over the descriptions of the surroundings
in which the events of the story take place, and the plot
structure, rather complex for Ōgai, is nicely worked out,
with Suezō the money lender and his wife serving as
comic and ironic foils for the romantic youngsters. Ōgai's
conscious use of symbols also marks a new development in
the evolution of his prose style. The two major symbols,
employed, in fact, transcend the novel. The image of the
protagonist shooting and killing a bird is repeated in the
play *The Ikuta River* and in his later story "Sahashi Jingorō."
The motif of the snake reoccurs in his story of the same
name. Whatever the implications of these symbols in the
totality of Ōgai's work, they function well in *Wild Goose*
and give a poetic dimension to the narrative at its two
high moments of tension. The basic situations of the novel
certainly grew out of Ōgai's own early experiences, and he
purposely cast them into an old-fashioned framework. Love
at first sight between a student and a young girl is a paradigm of much traditional fiction, especially in China; indeed, Ōgai includes in *Wild Goose* a number of significant
references to Chinese novels. Ōgai first imposes his own set
of images, based on his personal experience, on this larger
cultural myth, then transmutes his material to produce a
contemporary manifestation of a traditional situation,
through his use of psychological insights. In this context at
least the novel certainly deserves its generally high
reputation.

The last of the four novels, *Kaijin* (Destruction), begun
in 1912, is unfinished. The fragment of nineteen chapters
that remains is one of the most penetrating and unsettling
works in the whole canon of Ōgai's writing. Again Ōgai

uses various events from his own past as a means to provide the basic impetus for his narrative. A young man from the country comes to live with a wealthy family in the city. He wishes to become an intellectual and a writer himself. The tonality of the novel, however, is altogether different from that of *Youth.* Setsuzō, the protagonist, is moody and uncertain of himself, and there is a sense of strain in all the emotional relationships developed.

The general plot lines of the novel do not emerge in any very clear way from the finished portions that Ōgai finally published. The care with which he worked over the text is obvious, however. The first chapter in particular is a beautifully sustained piece of description. Setsuzō, now a middle-aged man, sets out to attend the funeral of a member of the family with which he once lived as a student and from which he now feels estranged. The grayness and general atmosphere of shabbiness conveyed, the sniveling priest, the dreary temple—all provide the proper emotional landscape for the protagonist's reflections and set the mood for what follows.

The remaining chapters provide a flashback to Setsuzō's student days, when he lived with the family. The political background of the period is indicated with some care (the family often discusses the implications of the Boxer Rebellion in China at the dinner table), and Ōgai's description of the house and the atmosphere of the rooms contains the sort of details that bring a sense of continuity and reality to the novel. Ōgai's care in composing his descriptions of the emotional reactions of the major characters is even greater. Setsuzō's is the most detailed portrait of all. It is by no means a flattering one.

He would somehow find a person attractive to him, then draw closer to examine him. Then, inevitably, at some point that person would disgust him. Usually it was precisely the point that first attracted Setsuzō that now turned him away. While

Setsuzō felt friendly, he was always kind and gentle and tended
to be conciliatory in everything. When the relationship was
over, he could be brutal and showed no humane concern of
any kind.[19]

Setsuzō is suspicious and jealous; as a child he listens to
a school mate play the flute; then one day, without knowing why, he enters his friend's room and smashes the instru-
ment. Setsuzō is a troubled person; yet even in his emotional
confusion, he never loses altogether the objective sense
of who he is.

Setsuzō realized that, in any emotional relationship with another person, there was a gap. In fact, he realized that he understood this very well. He knew that in the lives of others there
was something affirmative, so that in consonance with their
nature, they would look positively on something, no matter
what small differences in point of view there might be. He
could not adjust himself to this.[20]

Setsuzō despises others but wears a mask to hide his
real attitudes from them. He knows his technique is
successful.

Setsuzō's real attitudes were thus never communicated to
those around him. Indeed, most of them felt toward him a
real respect, tinged with awe. Others could not imagine that
he affirmed nothing and respected nothing; in fact they could
only suppose that his faith lay in things grand and lofty. Of
necessity they saw him as a man of great aspirations. Before
long, Setsuzō realized that he was surrounded by admirers.[21]

Like the doctor in Ōgai's drama *Masks*, Setsuzō assumes
an identity, but we are shown nothing positive, no life to
be saved, no germ to grow to fullfillment. The beginnings
of the plot that is developed concern the daughter of the
family, Otane, who finds herself stared at every day by a
curious young man who seems to be a hermaphrodite. Out
of morbid curiosity Setsuzō goes to talk to the young man,

who agrees to give up his attentions to Otane. The family mistakes Setsuzō's curiosity for loyalty and valor, and they think even more highly of him.

Setsuzō wishes to be a writer, and he thinks to take the hermaphrodite as a subject. His attitudes are quite different that those of Jun'ichi in *Youth*. "Just as a seagull flying in the sky looks beautiful," Setsuzō remarks to himself, "up close the bird looks gray and dingy. Beauty and goodness too, brought into close contact, are soiled and ugly. To show always the bright aspects of life in what one writes is to describe the brightness of a moment; to write of darkness is to tell the truth."[22]

The final section of the unfinished novel represents Setsuzō's first attempt to write. He creates a satire called "The Newspaper Country," in which everyone only makes, writes, and reads newspapers. Ōgai's satire represents in many ways a cruel and effective description of the evils he saw in contemporary Japanese society. In Newspaper County, all the jobs are interchangeable, and people take up politics in order to "create" news and hence newspaper articles. There is no trust and no individuality possible. Setsuzō comments that he was influenced in writing his satire by Poe's short story "The Devil in the Belfry," in which a mysterious stranger threatens to destroy a small self-satisfied German-speaking village. In a sense Setsuzō may be Ōgai's Devil, taking out his wrath on a society that refused to take cognizance of its own contradictions. The satire, unfortunately, seems to have little to do with the sections of the novel that precede it. Ōgai seems here to face an artistic problem crucial for writers in this century: how to integrate the personal and subjective with the realities of the objective world with which the writer is forced to deal. In the three novels Ōgai wrote before *Destruction,* the various elements were somehow connected; in this last and (from the evidence we have) most ambitious work of all, the strands simply fall apart.

Ōgai's sense of social malaise was reflected as well in a number of short works, often essays, written during the same three-year period, in which he comes to grips, intellectually and emotionally, with the darkening political climate. Two works in particular, "Shokudō" (The Dining Room) and "Chinmoku no tō" (The Tower of Silence), both written in 1910, provide important evidence of Ōgai's deeply troubled response to censorship and the restrictive measures taken toward socialism. They are not first-rate literary pieces but are compelling as cultural statements. More effective as literature is a 1912 short story "Nezumizaka" (Rat Hill), a kind of antiwar ghost story in which a man who raped and killed a woman in the Russo-Japanese War dies of fright after his acquaintance, a war profiteer grown rich and vulgar, tells the story at a party given to celebrate the building of his elaborate and tasteless new home.

Ōgai's major intellectual attempt to come to grips with the conflicts between the inner and the outer life came in the 1912 work "Ka no yō ni" (As If) and its shorter sequels. The story is little more than an essay in disguise, and the disguise is a familiar one: the protagonist, Hidemaro, has gone to Germany to study history and returns to find himself at variance with his wealthy father, who merely accepts certain customs of his own culture without understanding them. Conversations alternate between Hidemaro and his father, then Hidemaro and his friend, the artist Ayakoji. The two younger men have a relationship not unlike that of the two protagonists in Herman Hesse's novel *Narcissus and Goldmund,* in which artistic and intellectual facilities also are in debate. In Ōgai's case, the debate involves a discussion of the central idea expressed in an important contemporary work in German philosophy, *The Philosophy of As If,* published in 1911 by Hans Vaihinger (1852–1933), from which Ōgai took the title for his work. For a student of Ōgai's ideas, the discussions are revealing as an expression of his changing views of culture and history; in terms of Ōgai's growth as a writer, "As If" shows clearly the nature of his growing interest in history and what the study of history might accomplish as a means to reveal the ultimate nature of human values by transcending the present.

Hidemaro sets up as his life work the writing of a history of Japan in which he will make clear "the line that divides myth and history." He is determined to separate myth from fact. Fiction, like myth, he insists, is a kind of belief.

For example, a novel represents an untruth insofar as its purpose is regarded as presenting facts. But a novel is not accountable for this sort of truth but is indeed conceived of precisely in terms of such fabrication. Its very life exists in those fabrications. And its value. Sacred myths were conceived of in the same fashion; the only difference lies in the fact that the primal events of myth were considered to be true.[23]

Now, for Ōgai, both history and art can serve as liberating forces. Each can show a truth; combined, they can serve as a vehicle for his deepest commitments. The feeling for the need of a sense of personal history expressed at the conclusion of *Youth* and the despair Ōgai expressed over the state of his society in *Destruction* begin now to move toward a resolution. "As If" marks a major turning point in Ōgai's thought, the beginnings of a solution to the dilemmas he faced as a man and as an artist in the preceding years. When he began to write fiction again the following year, in 1912, he found the means to transcend his despair by looking backward in time.

CHAPTER 5

Man Transcending His Society, 1912 and After

THE period from 1912 until 1917, when Ōgai's health began to fail him, represents a culmination of his own philosophical consciousness and a final level of high success in his continuing endeavor to manifest his own understanding of the world in his artistic writings. In these last works Ōgai continues to pose new questions and to express new doubts, but now his art is conceived on a level of moral sensibility that goes deeper into the human condition than anything he wrote before.

Ōgai was able to expand his sensibility to this level by transcending his own problems and those of his immediate period. He turned to history for his subject matter, as he suggested he would at the end of *Youth* and in *As If*. These last writings range in content from closely reasoned factual accounts of particular events to philosophical *contes* in historical settings.

Ōgai's style is at its most perfect in these final works. His greatest gifts as a writer now combined: clarity of vision, a precise vocabulary, and the ability to suggest a transcendent meaning through recaptured fact. Idea and style finally join together. "If contemporary authors can write about life 'as it is' and readers find it satisfactory," wrote Ōgai in 1914, "they ought to appreciate a similar treatment of the past."[1] The purpose in writing these accounts was not merely to recreate the incidents they detail but to transcend them by suggesting through a recreation of the

96

specific incidents an intimation of the universal moral themes of which the incidents delineated serve as an example.

Grounded in the past as many of these works are, they are difficult for modern readers who may lack the background necessary to grasp the significance of certain details in the stories or to understand without some explanation the niceties of the moral choices that Ōgai propounds in them. The astonishing clarity of their style is obscured in translation. Nevertheless, for a reader who has the self-discipline to approach these literary texts with the same seriousness of purpose and intensity shown by their author, these works of Ōgai's last years will justify their reputation as the finest products of his insights into philosophy, history, and the human personality. They are texts to be meditated upon, not merely consumed. Read properly, they are thrilling.

Not all of the stories written during this period are historical. The 1913 story "Nagashi" (Back Scrubbing) and the 1915 story "Tenchō" (Heavenly Favor) in their separate ways, both deal with contemporary concepts of the meaning of art in society, and slighter pieces like "Yokyō" (Entertainment), also written in 1915, give both a satirical view of society and of the author himself. Nevertheless the great bulk of Ōgai's writing after 1912 uses history as a point of departure.

Ōgai's determination to use history as a means to transcend the contradictions he felt in his own society began when those contradictions were most strongly felt: the death of the Emperor Meiji in July, 1912, followed by the ritual suicide of General Nogi. Ōgai now took his first opportunity to examine a crisis in contemporary culture in historical terms. "The Last Will and Testament of Okitsu Yagoemon" was written in October, 1912, shortly after Nogi's suicide. The form and style of the story are unique in Ōgai's work; we are given in effect a dramatic mono-

logue, and Ōgai's work in the theater may have taught him
how to pace his narrative so effectively. Ōgai based his account on an actual ritual suicide by a retainer to the Hosokawa family, in the province of Higo in 1647. He creates
a suicide letter as it might have appeared at the period, in
elaborate Tokugawa language. (For this reason, the story
cannot make anything like its proper effect in a translation.) Ōgai's later historical works of the period are written with an outsider's detachment; here, by adopting the
first-person narrative technique, Ōgai was able to penetrate
the psychology of his historical protagonist to the point of
rendering credible the emotional attitudes leading to self-
destruction.

Okitsu killed another retainer in an argument over the
purchase of some rare goods for the Hosokawa family; he
was forgiven but felt that this act of clemency from his
master must be repaid. When his master died, Okitsu made
arrangements to commit ritual suicide. In the final passage
of his letter, he concludes, "unworthy though my own
station may be, I do not feel I will make an ignoble end.
As to this last testament, I leave it addressed to my son
Saiemon: son after son, grandson after grandson should
pass it down, succeeding in their turns to my aim. They
must excel in loyal devotion, in service to our noble house."[2]
Okitsu's straightforward simplicity of mind is its own
justification.

By composing "The Last Will and Testament of Okitsu
Yagoemon" in this fashion, Ōgai concealed his own emotional stance, and we are not given, except by the subtlest
of implications, Ōgai's own opinions as to the meaning
of such an act. His views are rendered more clearly in a
second story dealing with the subject of ritual suicide,
"The Abe Family," written a year later in 1913. Using another historical incident in which a number of members of
the Abe clan (also retainers to the family of Hosokawa)
committed suicide in 1641, Ōgai creates a grisly and emo-

tionally overwhelming account worthy of a Jacobean dramatist. He seems to suggest, from his detached position as narrator, that these men, so motivated to kill themselves, have been more concerned with the social rather than the spiritual significance of their deaths. In defining themselves in terms of society, they may have lost something of their own integrity. The code of behavior is followed, but at the individual's expense. "The Abe Family" is a first probing by Ōgai toward an understanding of the general meaning of human experience grounded in the specifics of time and place.

Ōgai's historical accounts and stories examine the whole range of Japanese history. Two of the most impressive have to do with the beginning of the Meiji period, the time of Ōgai's own childhood. "Sakai jiken" (The Incident at Sakai), written in 1914, is an assessment of a celebrated incident of 1868, in which the French demanded the ritual suicide of twenty men as a reparation for a scuffle between French and Japanese soldiers at the port of Sakai, near Osaka. The new government, anxious to avoid any possible war with a foreign power, acceded to these demands. Ōgai again focuses his attention on the mentality of the men who are to die for a code of honor that, like the code in "The Abe Family," was growing obsolescent. "The Incident at Sakai" is full of fascinating detail, including a description of the queasiness felt by the French officials who were forced to watch the Japanese soldiers disembowel themselves. All the events crowding the story serve to illustrate Ōgai's conception of the relentlessness of historical change. The doomed men in the story are victims in every way, and, as victims, they have a tragic dignity.

A second story, "Tsuge Shirōzaemon," written in 1915, provides another examination of the ironies of history. In 1869, Tsuge Shirōzaemon assassinated Yokoi Shōnan, a leading thinker and political figure of the day who, in his moderate and enlightened way, hoped to open Japan to foreign influence. Ōgai came to compose the account after having met Tsuge's son, who was a friend of his brother. Ōgai felt a melancholy concern for the man whose father had committed a terrible crime for what he thought was the right reason, yet whose meaningless act merely showed the terrible ambivalence of all human values before the inevitable forces of historical change.

The bulk of Ōgai's historical accounts, however, is set in the Tokugawa period (1600–1868), the time in which Japanese social and spiritual values were firmly set in patterns that were of fundamental importance even to the men of Ōgai's generation. The Tokugawa stories represent a probing of Ōgai's own spiritual past in terms of the society that made it. These works range from accounts based on meticulous historical research to short pieces of fiction. In subject matter, they are often ingenious. The 1913 story "Sahashi Jingorō," for example, deals with the counterplay of cunning between Jingorō and Tokugawa Ieyasu, the founder of the Tokugawa dynasty. Ōgai opens the story with the arrival of the Korean envoys in 1604, who come hoping to resume relations with Japan after a period of interruptions following the Japanese invasion of Korea under Hideyoshi. The narrative is then developed in a series of flashbacks. Jingorō's shooting of a bird, mentioned earlier in connection with a similar scene in *Wild Goose*, marks the beginning of his moral downfall. Later, Jingorō's lack of moral fortitude on several occasions serves as a theme that unites the colorful incidents of the story.

Moral pressure remains the impetus behind the events in a long story written the following year, "Kuriyama Daizen." The extremely complex events of the narrative, possibly based on research begun by Ōgai during his period of "exile" in Kyushu, concern a misdemeanor committed in 1632 by Kuroda Tadayuki, the head of a powerful clan in the Fukuoka area. Ōgai concentrates his attention on one

of Tadayuki's retainers, Kuriyama Daizen Toshiaki, whose
grasp of the moral implications of the situation cause him,
at great danger to his own career, to lie to the authorities
in order to force his master to come to his senses.

The actual text of the story is almost wholly factual. The
reader is presented with a number of historical personages who face a political and a moral problem. The narrative eventually indicates how the problem was solved,
and, by implication, the nature of obligation and loyalty
in the highest sense. Ōgai the commentator or narrator
never intrudes. What then is the artistry involved? Ōgai's
highly successful technique here is *selectivity*. Only those
details that further the purposes of the story are provided;
all other information is omitted. Some of the material is
created: small touches revealing of personality are added,
conversations are imagined, unrelated incidents are juxtaposed to emphasize the moral thrust of the narrative. Ōgai
does not commence his account at its logical beginning—
this information is later provided by flashbacks—but at the
time of the first serious philosophical confrontation between
the lord Kuroda Tadayuki and his retainer Kuriyama Daizen Toshiaki. In the early sections of the story, the reader
sees Toshiaki through his lord's disparaging eyes. Toshiaki's
conduct thus looks suspicious. As more detail is provided,
however, and Lord Tadayuki's erratic behavior is confirmed,
the reader's opinion is subtly shifted to the point where
he is faced with the same set of moral dilemmas as Toshiaki.
He eventually defies his lord, is taken to Edo, and called
before the magistrates. By this point in the long (and
complicated) narrative, the reader is able to look objectively at all those sitting in the courtroom and, rather than
siding emotionally with any one group of those present,
focus his attention on the moral and philosophical differences between a higher and a lower loyalty. Surprisingly,
this objectivity conveys to the reader a tremendous emotional force and a sense of grandeur that far transcends the

incident described. Selectivity has made this result possible.

Man is what he does, Ōgai seems to be saying in "Kuri-yama Daizen"; even in a slight piece like the 1917 "Tokō Tahei," he can examine the few remaining records of a minor retainer in the house of Hosokawa (as was Okitsu Yagoemon) to find a man who, in his instinctive responses to the situations in which he finds himself, gives evidence of great personal integrity. Some of the situations are subtle ones, involving Zen and swordsmanship or Tahei's re-sponses to accusations of thievery in Edo. Tahei's attitudes, wrote Ōgai, represent a conviction that he must always be prepared to face death. "To be willing to die is no doubt a straightforward attitude of mind," Ōgai comments, "never-theless, it seems that among samurai those who had such a will, no matter during what period, in no matter what domain, were not so easy to find."[3]

In "Tokō Tahei" Ōgai spends considerable time sifting the scanty evidence he has put before the reader. He raises questions and he refuses to interject mere supposition. Con-cerning a possible meeting between Tahei and the legendary swordsman Miyamoto Musashi, Ōgai writes:

... at least I would like to think it happened that way. If I were writing a novel, I could merely write that it was so and not waste words in the fashion I have.

I have here exposed to view the conventional sort of mech-anisms brought to bear on what is usually termed the historical novel. Historians, seeing what I have written, will no doubt criticize me for my willfulness. Novelists, on the other hand, will laugh at my persistence. There is a Western proverb about sleeping between two beds. Looking at my own work, it seems that this proverb can be applied to me.[4]

Stories like "Tokō Tahei" and "Kuriyama Daizen" or the long 1914 story "Ōshio Heihachirō," an account of the life and suicide of the Confucian reformer, seem close to historical fact; Ōgai's "willfulness," if any, is in his selection and arrangement of events in order to bring out their moral underpinnings, as it were. A story like the touching "Yasui Fujin" (Yasui's Wife), written in 1914, is closer perhaps to fiction. Ōgai's interest in the Confucian scholar Yasui Sokken (1799–1876) lay not so much in his philosophical ideas as in how he lived his life, and by what means the virtues he studied—prudence, humanity, kindness—became a part of his personality by the refining of his own temperament through his marriage to Sayo, a remarkable woman who appreciated her short, pockmarked, and impecunious husband for his real attributes of seriousness and compassion. In his construction of the narrative, Ōgai does not hesitate to create conversations, characters, and episodes that move his narrative into the realm of fiction. He also permits himself, as an objective outsider, to comment on the events and attitudes he recounts. His speculations on Sayo's real character mark in many ways the high point of the story.

She was surely not so foolish that she did not understand what luxury was, nor could she have been so selfless as to have no needs or desires for anything physical or spiritual. In fact Sayo did seem to have had one uncommon desire, before which all else was only dust and ashes to her. What was her desire? It was that the intelligent persons of society would say that she had hoped for the distinction of her husband. I who write this cannot deny it. Yet on the other hand, I cannot crudely agree with the view that she merely gave her labors and her patience to her husband like some merchant who has invested capital for profit but dies before any recompense could come.

Sayo surely had a dream, some image of the future. Until her death, did not the look in her beautiful eyes seem fixed on some far, far place; or was it that she had no leisure even to feel that her own death might be unfortunate? Was not the very object of her hope something that she never precisely clarified for herself?[5]

Ōgai's speculations suddenly bridge the gap between Yasui's wife and ourselves; and as we follow the movements of the author's mind, we are inevitably moved just as he has prepared us to be. We are moved because we have understood Sayo, not merely because we have reacted emotionally to her presence in the story. The kind of grave, reflective poignancy Ōgai creates in "Yasui's Wife" is the hallmark of his late style.

Sayo's nobility of character and her acceptance of what she could not know gives her more than a passing resemblance to characters in several other of Ōgai's Tokugawa pieces. "Jiisan baasan" (The Old Man and the Old Woman), written in 1915, also tells the story of a husband and wife: he is impetuous, she accepting, even of his faults. The couple, separated by a misdemeanor of the husband, are reunited in old age to share their mutual contentment.

> In every way the two seemed to live a life appropriate to retirement, one of unhurried leisure. The old man would put on his eyeglasses and read his books. He kept a diary in fine script. Every morning at the same time he would polish his swords. He kept in good physical condition by practicing strokes with a wooden sword. The old lady continued as if she were a little girl playing house, and in her spare moments she would come to the old man's side to cool him with her fan. The weather was gradually becoming warmer. After she fanned him for awhile, the old man would put down the book he had been reading and begin to speak with her. Their conversations always seemed to be very pleasant.[6]

In "The Old Man and the Old Woman," this reciprocal calm has been earned; in "Yasui's Wife" it is given but nurtured and sustained. In "Saigo no ikku" (The Last Phrase), written in 1915, the heroine, a girl of sixteen named Ichi has the same quiet self-determination as her spiritual sisters in these other stories, but she is forced to take a public stand. Her father was condemned to be beheaded as a thief, and in an effort to save him, she eventually defies the highest authorities. Her quiet convictions are unshakable. Thus she becomes a subversive, a dangerous figure.

At this period the officials of the Tokugawa family had no idea of the Western word "martyr," nor was the word "self-sacrifice" in the dictionaries of the time. So it was no wonder that, as no distinction in the human spirit was made between old or young, man or woman, they did not understand the kind of behavior shown by the daughter of the criminal Tarobe. Yet Sasa, who had talked with Ichi, was not the only one to be pierced by the spirit of rebellion lurking within her attitude of self-sacrifice, for it cut into the hearts of the others in the hall as well.[7]

Rebellion in self-sacrifice, the freedom shown by one who, by submitting, calls into question the canons on which authority is based: these themes, first sounded lightly in the German stories written twenty-five years before, now come to the fore in the full clarity of Ōgai's mature vision. He has taken the emotional truth from the romantic European surroundings and developed it into a moral image that, grounded in the Japanese past as it is, is wholly his own and yet altogether universal.

Rebellion and authority play an important part in one of Ōgai's most lyrical and justly loved stories set in the Tokugawa period, "Takasebune" (The Boat on the River Takase), written in 1915. Here, all the elements in Ōgai's art seem in perfect balance. Accurate observation of historical detail is combined with an acute perception of human moral psychology, both revealed in a precise yet poetic style.

The boat carries a criminal, a young man accused of murdering his brother. For the most part, the story represents an exchange between Kisuke, the innocent "criminal" who nevertheless submits, and the constable Haneda Shōbē, who, wedded to his own materialistic mentality, has difficulty in looking beyond his own unexamined ideas to the question of moral values larger than judicial innocence or guilt. As he hears Kisuke's story, however, his thoughts are forced to expand despite himself.

He began to reflect on man's life in general. When a man is ill, he wishes he were well. When he never eats properly day after day, he can only wish for enough to eat. When he has no money set aside for an emergency, he wishes he had something saved up. If he has some, he wishes he had more. After all, one thing leads to another, and there was no telling when a man would finally draw the line. Yet right before his eyes he saw the living example of one who had drawn this line—Kisuke.[8]

Kisuke is a desperately poor young man who has struggled, along with his brother, to eke out a meager livelihood. In a fit of despair the brother tries to commit suicide but fails; Kisuke, hoping to end his brother's agony as quickly as possible, pulls the knife from his brother's throat but is seen, then accused of murder. Even though he knows his own innocence he is ultimately willing to accept the judgment, because he was able to bring peace to his brother.

When Shōbē learns the details of Kisuke's story, he realizes the young man is innocent. Yet he lacks the courage to pursue his realization.

After thinking over the various aspects of the problem, Shōbē came to the conclusion that all he could do was leave the problem to the judgment of those above; all he could do was to go along with authority. He decided to make the judgment of the magistrate his own. Yet despite his decision, he still felt ill at ease and wished that somehow, he might find the means to discuss the case again with the magistrate.

The gloomy night continued until the end, and the boat with its two quiet occupants slid softly over the dark waters.[9]

The inevitability of the concluding sentence produces a special pathos found in the best of these historical narratives. The same emotions are even more beautifully rendered in a long story written in the same year. "Sanshō dayū" (Sanshō the Bailiff), is for many Ōgai's masterpiece, with its superbly sustained atmosphere and a whole cast of characters who manifest in full measure the moral qualities Ōgai examined in previous accounts. "Sanshō the Bailiff" is not set in the Tokugawa period but is Ōgai's sole attempt at recreating a legend from the medieval period. Perhaps the lack of actual historical detail available to him, plus the slight aura of mystery surrounding the story, permitted him to expand his own imagination to an unusual level of sustained lyric sensibility.

The story concerns two children, the girl Anju and her younger brother Zushiō. While on a journey to search out their father, who has been banished to Southern Japan for a supposed political crime, the children and their mother fall prey to slave traders, who separate the two youngsters from their mother and sell all three into slavery. The children are eventually sold to Sanshō, and much of the story revolves around their learning to live in the confines of the camp, sustained by their love for each other and for their missing parents. Anju decides that they must escape. Like Ichi in "The Last Phrase," Anju's attitudes are a blend of self-sacrifice and rebellion; she helps her brother to escape, then drowns herself to resist torture. After various vicissitudes, Zushiō, who becomes a man of power and rank, searches on and on for his mother, until he finds her.

Without knowing precisely why, he was attracted to something in the woman. He stopped and looked inside the hedge. The woman's unkempt hair was clotted with dust. When he looked at her face, he saw she was blind, and a strong surge of pity for her went through him. As the moments passed, he began to understand the words of the little song she was muttering to herself. His body trembled as if he had a fever, and tears welled up in his eyes. For these were the words the woman was repeating over and over to herself:

> My Anju, I yearn for you.
> > Fly away!
> My Zushiō, I yearn for you.
> > Fly away!
> Little birds, if you are living still,
> > Fly, fly far away!
> I will not chase you.

He stood transfixed, enraptured by her words. Suddenly his whole body seemed on fire: he had to grit his teeth to hold back the animal scream welling up within him. As though freed from invisible chains, he rushed through the hedge. Trampling on the millet grains, he threw himself at the feet of the woman. The amulet, which he had been holding up in his right hand, pushed against his forehead when he threw himself on the ground.

The woman realized that something bigger than a sparrow had come storming into the millet. She stopped her endless song and stared ahead of her with her blind eyes. Then, like dried seashells swelling open in water, her eyes began to moisten and open.

"Zushiō!" she called out. They rushed into each other's arms.[10]

The story ends here, in the full force of Ōgai's moral lyricism.

Not all of the historical stories are set in Japan. Two in particular are based on Chinese models; one, "Kanzan Jittoku," written in 1915, is a beautifully laconic retelling of the legend of the great Han Shan, the legendary figure in Ch'an (Zen) Buddhism whose Cold Mountain poems have become well known in recent years through excellent translations by Gary Snyder and Burton Watson. A second, "Gyogenki," written in the same year, is an account of the T'ang dynasty Taoist nun and poetess Yü Hsüan-chi.

In addition to the historical stories written during these years Ōgai wrote three long accounts of historical personages in the Tokugawa period. The first of them, *Shibue Chūsai* (1916), is a reconstruction of the life of a doctor in the late Tokugawa period. The second, *Izawa Ranken* (1916), goes on to investigate the life of Chūsai's teacher Ranken, and the third, *Hōjō Katei*, which takes up the career of his acquaintance Hōjō Katei, written in 1917, pushes back the chronology still further.

For many discerning Japanese readers, these three works, especially *Shibue Chūsai*, represent Ōgai's supreme accomplishment. Even more than the stories, these three works serve as the means he chose to create his own link with the totality of reality as he understood it; and in doing so, he wrote his spiritual autobiography. Chūsai, like Ōgai, was a doctor in the service of the state and a great lover of the arts, especially of the theater.

Chūsai was a physician and a bureaucrat. He studied books of philosophy on various aspects of Confucianism, he read history, and he studied in the field of the arts as well, literature and poetry. In this regard we resemble each other very closely indeed. Still, one noticeable difference is that, putting aside the fact that we lived at different times, our lives have not had precisely the same value. No, in fact, I must admit there is one enormous difference. Although Chūsai was able to establish himself as a real student in philosophy and in art, I have not been able to escape from my own vague world of the dilettante. Looking at Chūsai, I can only feel a sense of shame.

Chūsai was indeed a man who walked the same road that I have. Yet his stride was something I could never hope to imitate. He was vastly superior to me in every way. I owe him all my respect. Indeed, the extraordinary thing is that he walked not only all the great roads but came and went by the byways as well. Not only did he study neo-Confucianism, but he amused himself with books of heraldry and old maps of Edo. If Chūsai had been my contemporary, our sleeves surely would have rubbed as we walked through those muddy lanes. An intimacy would have developed between us. And I would have come to love him.[11]

Ōgai searched out obscure records for details on Chūsai's life, visited abandoned temples to locate graves, checked accounts with one scholar after another. The accumulation of detail is relentless, and eventually a portrait of the person and the times emerges that, given the relative obscurity of those whose lives and careers are being examined, seems extraordinarily complete.

Ōgai's appearance here as editor and commentator is the final development in his objectifying technique that began in his earliest stories and continued in works like "The Tale of a Hundred Candles." In *Shibue Chūsai*, many of the historical materials serve as a kind of objective correlative to Ōgai's sense of his own spiritual autobiography. Ōgai does not merely read himself back into history; he finds in these men ideals and emotional attitudes that forge strong links between their generation and his own. Ōgai finds himself able to compare himself directly with Chūsai, and, in terms of the standards he uses, finds himself wanting. He faces the past directly and with courage. *Shibue Chūsai* and the two later accounts, however, are exceedingly difficult for a modern reader to penetrate, as he must arm himself with a tremendous amount of explanatory material in order to understand the bare meaning of the texts. Here the mass of detail is not softened by conversations or descriptions; and, while the grasp of minute, objective particular (dates, locations of homes, names of friends, puzzling discrepancies in official records) does provide the individual details that make up Ōgai's grand design, the pattern may be hard to see. For all but the most determined readers, the total meaning of Ōgai's search for roots in this confrontation with history in *Shibue Chūsai* may have to be accepted as an article of faith.

From the examination of his most personal experience in his early work, Ōgai's artistic universe expanded to enormous proportions by the time he composed these last biographies. By moving away in time toward a level of generalization based on other cultural and social circumstances than those prevalent in Japan at the end of World War I, Ōgai found the means to take to task his own time, not because it failed to live up to the past (Ōgai's view of the past was by no means sentimental) but because those who ought to understand the importance in any age of the need for virtue and for self-fulfillment seemed blind to such an imperative. In many ways Ōgai, like his heroines Anju and Ichi, was a rebel who bowed to an authority he respected no more than Sanshō or the Tokugawa judge.

Some Japanese critics have maintained that Ōgai turned away from writing about contemporary life because he found it too difficult to comprehend or because he was too fatigued to find the energy to grasp the meaning of the changes that were coming to Japan. The evidence seems to show something quite different. The themes of the historical stories invariably have a contemporary significance. Ōgai's interest in modern European literature continued unabated, and the numerous translations he made after 1912 included the newest works by such writers as Schnitzler, Gorki, Rilke, and Hofmannsthal. And indeed Ōgai's choice of material to translate often seems dictated by his own artistic concerns at the time. Strindberg's play of 1907, *Storm Weather*, which he translated in 1915, involves the treatment of the same themes of rebellion and authority that Ōgai was writing about himself, and the attitudes of the protagonist might be those in one of Ōgai's stories.

GENTLEMAN: People can't stand independence— they want you to obey them. All my subordinates—even the watchman in the factory—wanted me to obey

> them. And if I wouldn't, they called me a
> despot. . . . The maids in the house wanted me
> to obey them—eat warmed-over food—and when
> I wouldn't, they egged my wife on against me
> . . . my wife wanted me to obey the child—I
> walked out. . . . Then they all conspired against
> the tyrant—that was me![12]

Ōgai's greatest translations, however, were his versions
of Shakespeare's *Macbeth* (from the German translation
by Heinrich Vos) and Goethe's *Faust*, both finished in
1913. In rendering these two masterpieces into his own language, Ōgai prepared himself by this final apprenticeship
with these two great writers to examine his own life and
society from an ambitious perspective. In his later years
Ōgai had come to revere Goethe enormously, and the
homage he paid by translating the German poet's greatest
work helped him expand his own artistic and moral per-
spectives to the level revealed in his last writings.

Ōgai also translated in 1913 Goethe's early play *Götz
von Berlichingen*, which he, like so many others, admired
for its sweep and energy. In one important passage, Götz,
imprisoned in his castle, talks with his retainers.

ALL: Freedom forever!
GÖTZ: And, if that survive us, we can die happy; for our
          spirits shall see our children's children and their
          emperor happy! Did the servants of princes show the
          same filial attachment to their masters as you to me—
          did their masters serve the emperor as I serve him. . . .
GEORGE: Things would be widely different.
GÖTZ: Not so much as it would appear. Have I not known
          worthy men among the princes? And can the race be
          extinct? Men, happy in their own minds and in their
          subjects, who could bear a free, noble brother in their
          neighborhood without harboring either fear or envy;
          whose neighborhood expanded when they saw their
          table surrounded by their free equals, and who did

not think the knights unfit companions until they had degraded themselves by courtly homage.

GEORGE: Have you known such princes?

GÖTZ: Ay, truly. As long as I live I shall recollect how the Landgrave of Hanau gave a grand hunting party, and the princes and the free feudatories dined under the open heaven, and all the country people thronged to see them: it was no selfish masquerade instituted for his own private pleasure or vanity. To see them all, merry as if they rejoiced in the spendor of their master, which he shared with them under God's free sky![13]

This vision of order and spiritual health painted here by Goethe seems close to the heart of the moral world Ōgai invoked in his own last works that reflect, as they do, on authority, personal honor, and the meaning of integrity. Ōgai, it would seem, did not retreat into the past but rather transcended the present.

CHAPTER 6

Some Observations on Ōgai's Work

MORI Ōgai, as this brief study hopefully has helped to show, deserves the reputation as a major figure in twentieth-century cultural and artistic history that the Japanese have given him. Critical opinion there has stressed his resolution to grasp and disseminate Western ideas, especially in German literature and philosophy. Japanese scholars also credit him, along with Futabatei Shimei, with introducing Western modes of psychological expression into Japanese literature, and with successfully enlarging the scope of Japanese fiction to include intellectual and philosophical themes once reserved for poetry and essays. The themes of his stories, indeed, often deal either with Western subjects, such as the early German tales, or with themes seldom taken up in the traditional Japanese literature of artistic merit—the psychology of marital discord, for example, or the relationships between political and personal malaise. Even the historical stories treat their material in an analytical fashion altogether different from the way in which a Tokugawa writer of historical tales—Ueda Akinari, for example—might have done.

Ōgai's early exposure to the West and his scientific training are the reasons usually given for his detached and candid attitudes of mind. While this is surely true, a Western reader would have to comment as well that Ōgai, in both his early education and general temperament, belonged to the last generation of Japanese reared in the Tokugawa

Confucian tradition of self-sacrifice, hard work, and dedication to duty. For Ōgai there was always a high moral
purpose involved in the act of writing, and in the act of
living. This sense of purpose propelled him into following
his father in service through medicine. Many writers in the
late nineteenth and early twentieth century, in that period
of enormous social change, were physicians. Lu Hsün,
the most respected writer of modern China, studied medicine in Japan at the turn of the century, then returned to
China to educate his contemporaries. The brilliant Philip-
pine novelist José Rizal studied medicine in Madrid in the
1880s. He returned to Manila to write a scathing denun-
ciation of the Spanish colonial regime, in his novel *Noli
me tangere*, then suffer martyrdom by execution. Chekhov,
in Russia, continued to practice medicine and write of the
changes in his society with a detachment not unlike that
of Ōgai.

These men, for various reasons, had a high sense of the
moral possibilities of literature, and their work shows their
ability to combine a certain objectivity of spirit with their
private and honest human responses to their own society.
The works of literature that resulted, although different in
style in the case of each writer, all evoke a sense of high
purpose. Certain resemblances in form might also be
noted. In describing Chekhov, the critic V. S. Pritchett
reminds us that "the mark of genius is an incessant activity
of mind," and then goes on to say:

> Medicine, he said, was his wedded wife, and literature his
> mistress: he is very much the man who chases two hares at
> once, though medical experience enriched his writing. One
> also suspects that Chekhov's worry about "purpose" had a
> good deal to do with his inability to write a long novel; he
> could not sustain a philosophic plan.[1]

The relentlessness of the objective intellect and the
pressure of events—these were what kept Chekhov from

making the commitment to reserve for himself the mental and spiritual time for reflection necessary for lengthy artistic creation. The same situation held true for Lu Hsün and for Ōgai himself, who felt bound by reality, contemporary or historical, and thus never found it possible to create large artistic structures. In his late 1917 essay, "From my Ledger," Ōgai explained that his love for the facts of history was not something that came to him late in his career as some Japanese critics have suggested, but from his earliest responses to life; his training in science only reaffirmed these first attitudes of mind. Commenting on the denseness of his last biographies Ōgai concludes that "... the fact that I have moved toward the use of these spare genealogies may well lie in the momentum of scientific spirit behind the pursuit of such relationships in Zola's *Les Rougon-Macquart*."[2] Ōgai first wrote of Zola in 1892; twenty-five years later he had come to terms with one aspect of Zola's own sense of the objective; yet Ōgai's own Apollonian view of his literary craft, permitted him to move beyond documentation to the point where his works bear no resemblance to those of the French writer at all.

Ōgai's high sense of purpose as a writer also led him to assume other roles appropriate to the Confucian artistic and intellectual tradition. His translations pay homage to the great Western classics, just as deference had been paid to the Chinese writers until the generation before. Ōgai's essay writing, his help in founding poetry magazines, and his work in the theater all were carried on, usually at a high cost of energy and mental leisure, because of his dedication to the truth of the future. His work however, for all its moral purpose, strikes at a far deeper level than that of mere ideology. His political stance (seldom directly expressed, sometimes changing) is at best an ambiguous clue to his real purposes. In this regard, Chekhov's remarks might well have been made by Ōgai:

It's not conservatism I'm balancing off with liberalism—they are not at the heart of the matter as far as I am concerned—it's the lies of my heroes with their truths. . . . You told me once my stories lack an element of protest, and that they have neither sympathies nor antipathies. But doesn't the story protest against lying from start to finish? Isn't that ideology? . . . a writer is a man bound by contract to his duty and his conscience.[3]

Above and beyond Ōgai's significance in the context of Japanese literary history, his life and work have a peculiar fascination for the Western reader as well. On one level they provide a perfect case study in the realm of art and ideas for differentiating between Westernization and modernization in Japanese culture, as well as providing a means to examine a typical pattern among modern Japanese intellectuals of an early exposure to Western influence brought back and amalgamated into the totality of their grasp of their own culture. These problems in intellectual history are fascinating ones that have not yet been fully understood, let alone solved.

Charles Baudelaire's notes for an unfinished article entitled "Philosophic Art," written in the late 1850s, begins with the definition of pure art as ". . . the creation of an evocative magic, containing at once the object and the subject, the world external to the artist and the artist himself."[4] Yet less than a century later the Austrian Marxist critic T. W. Adorno was able to write persuasively concerning what he saw as the inevitable, irrevocable split in the modern consciousness between subject, one's own subjective view of oneself, and object, the objective nature of the world and its forces to which the individual is subjected. Frederic Jameson, in writing of Adorno, says that ". . . the novel is always an attempt to reconcile the consciousness of the writer and reader with the world at large; so it is that the judgments we make on the great novelists fall not on them, but on the moment of history which they reflect and on which their structures pass sentence."[5] One

need not accept the entire proposition to agree that the
precarious balance between an inner view of reality and
the ever more impersonal mechanisms of society is threatened by forces that seem bent on destroying the humane
quality of wholeness that has been valued throughout time.
For Adorno, there is a desperate courage involved in
"imagining wholeness in a period that has no experience
of it."[6]

During Ōgai's lifetime, Japan was fast losing that sense
of wholeness. Examined from Adorno's perspective, Ōgai
tried at times to write of the objective world, sometimes
of the individual psyche. In *Youth* he managed to maintain
some balance between the two. In *Destruction*, he could
no longer relate the two elements, and we are given the two
fragments—pieces of the protagonist's spiritual world and
a satire on contemporary Japanese society. In Ōgai's final
historical and synthetic works, his courage to show wholeness, as Adorno would have it, called for superb artistic con-
trol and a tremendous outlay of moral energy.

Ōgai is not an easy writer to read. To appreciate him on
the literary level, one must know something of the
traditions of Chinese, Japanese, and German literature, both
in poetry and prose. To appreciate the import of the questions he poses, one must know German philosophy and
Confucianism as well. To sense the power of his work,
one must be willing to follow various elevents in his thought
through form after form, work after work, as Ōgai moves
toward the kind of synthesis he achieved in certain works
of his last years.

In the best of Ōgai's works, style and content are really
impossible to separate: one dictates the other. Precedents
can be found, of course, for certain aspects of his writing,
in Chinese historical models or in German nineteenth-
century writers like Nietzsche, where the flow of ideas
can carry a narrative along. Yet Ōgai's works do not resemble his models, the rhythm of his sentences and the

subtle juxtapositions of incident make the form and style he evolved uniquely his own. Any judgments on the artistic success of any given work must be made on the basis of rules peculiar to it, rules that must be gleaned from a close examination of, and a reflection on, that individual text. Ōgai was an artist and a philosopher; he was a fine writer because one set of sensibilities consistently refreshed and enriched the other.

Notes and References

Abbreviations:

MOZ   *Mori Ōgai zenshū* (The Complete Works of Mori Ōgai), 8 volumes (Tokyo: Chikuma Shobo, 1971).
MN   *Monumenta Nipponica*
OZ   *Ōgai zenshū* (The Complete Works of Ōgai), 38 volumes (Tokyo: Iwanami shoten, 1972).

I have quoted from a number of translations of Ōgai's works already available; those without citation are my own.

Chapter One

1. Ōgai's remarks are made at the beginning of a late story, *Saiki Koi*, written in 1917. (*MOZ*, 4:266.) All the authors mentioned enjoyed great reputations until the end of the nineteenth century, especially Takizawa Bakin (1767–1848), whose grandiose and moralistic novels, often based on Chinese models, gave him a reputation not unlike Sir Walter Scott in Great Britain at the same period. Santō Kyōden (1761–1816) also wrote popular novels, some satirical, some didactic. Tamenaga Shunsui (1790–1840) and Shōtei Kinsui (1795–1862) both wrote popular novels, sometimes of an erotic character.

2. A quotation from the autobiographic story "Mōsō (Delusion), written in 1911. *MOZ*, 2:125–26.

3. This English rendering of the Japanese version of Gray's "Elegy" can be found on page 134 of Donald Keene's *Landscapes and Portraits* (Tokyo and Palo Alto: Kodansha, 1971) in his authoritative essay, "Modern Japanese Poetry."

4. *MOZ*, 7:69.

5. For a stimulating discussion of the modernization of the Japanese language, see Marleigh Ryan, *Japan's First Modern Novel: Ukigumo* (New York: Columbia University Press, 1967), pp. 80–95.

6. *MOZ*, 3:279.

7. *MOZ*, 7:99.

8. Unfortunately there is not, at this writing, a full translation available of Sōseki's *And Then*. The quotation is from Edwin McClellan, *Two Japanese Novelists* (Chicago: Chicago University Press, 1969), p. 37.

9. *MOZ*, 7:105.

10. *Ibid.*, pp. 109–10.

11. *Ibid.*, p. 112.

Chapter Two

1. *MOZ*, 1:5. The translation quoted here is by Leon Zolbrod from "The Girl Who Danced," in M. A. Martin, ed., *The Language of Love* (Bantam Books, 1964), p. 3.

2. *Ibid.*, p. 16. The translation is by Zolbrod, p. 14.

3. Hans Christian Andersen, *The Improvisatore*, translated by Mary Howitt (London: Ward, Lock and Company, n.d. [c. 1857]), p 165.

4. *Ibid.*, p. 166.

5. *Ibid.*, pp. 252–53.

6. *Ibid.*, p. 258.

7. The Japanese text is in *MOZ*, 8:18.

Chapter Three

1. *OZ*, 5:576.

2. *Ibid.*, p. 583. Saigyō (1118–1190) was a monk and the greatest poet of his age.

3. *Ibid.*, p. 584.

4. *Ibid.*, p. 586. The translation cited here is the fine one by Helen Craig McCullough on page 234 of her version of the *Giheiki*, retitled in English *Yoshitsune* (Stanford: Stanford University Press, 1966).

5. *Ibid.*, p. 587.

6. *MOZ*, 7:226.

7. *Ibid.*, p. 272.

8. *OZ*, 19:429.

9. *Ibid.*, p. 455.

Chapter Four

1. *MOZ*, 1:71. The English version quoted here is from a translation of the story by John Dower, *MN*, 26 (1971), 133.

2. *Ibid.*, p. 72. The translation is from Dower, p. 134.

3. *Ibid.*, p. 245. The English version here is from a translation by Ivan Morris in *Modern Japanese Stories* (Rutland, Vt. and Tokyo: Tuttle, 1962), p. 39.

4. *Ibid.*, p. 74. The translation is from Dower, pp. 136–37.

5. *Ibid.*, p. 216.

6. *Ibid.*, p. 68. The English version quoted here is from a translation by Darcy Murray in *MN*, 28 (1973), 359.

7. For a fascinating account of the real Hanako and her relations with Rodin, see "Hanako" in Donald Keene's *Landscapes and Portaits*, pp. 250–58.

8. *MOZ*, 1:263.

9. *Ibid.*, p. 272.

10. *MOZ*, 2:170.

11. *MOZ*, 1:135. The quotation is from the translation by Ninomiya and Goldstein, *Vita Sexualis* (Rutland, Vt. and Tokyo: Tuttle, 1972), pp. 103–4.

12. *Ibid.*, p. 140. The translation is from Ninomiya/Goldstein, p. 117.

13. *Ibid.*, p. 154. The translation is from Ninomiya/Goldstein, p. 152.

14. *MOZ*, 2:113.

15. *Ibid.*, p. 35.

16. *Ibid.*, p. 64.

17. *Ibid.*, p. 111.

18. *MOZ*, 3:41. The quotation is from the translation by Ochiai and Goldstein, *The Wild Geese* (Rutland, Vt. and Tokyo: Tuttle, 1959), pp. 76–77.

19. *MOZ*, 2:187.

20. *Ibid.*, p. 190.

21. *Ibid.*, pp. 190–91.

22. *Ibid.*, p. 206.

23. *Ibid.*, p. 247.

Chapter Five

1. *MOZ*, 7:105.

2. *MOZ*, 3:104.

3. *MOZ*, 4:237.

4. *Ibid.*, p. 233.

5. *MOZ*, 3:229–30.

6. *Ibid.*, pp. 265–66.

7. *Ibid.*, p. 279.

8. *Ibid.*, p. 283.

9. *Ibid.*, p. 287.

10. *Ibid.*, pp. 253–54. The image of a blind woman seems to have been an important one to Ōgai. A preliminary sketch for this scene is tucked into the text of "Half a Day," written in 1909.

One day as he passed the granary he noticed an old woman in the shop. She was one of those old women whose white hair had grown yellow and whose hands were as wrinkled as crushed oil paper. She would place a fistful of small red beans in the flat of her hand and pick out particles of dust and shells. It had caught his attention and he stood there watching for a minute. Then he had begun to think. The shop had a big pile of grain to winnow and so there was a lot of husks. It seemed to be the old woman's job to take a handful of them at a time and, peering with her old blurred eyes, she would pick out the particles. But she was really superfluous, for a servant boy was shaking a large bamboo winnowing basket by her side. And yet for all that the old woman was wrapped up in what she was doing.

The text is in *MOZ*, 1:66. The translation is from the Darcy version. See note 10, chapter 4.

11. *MOZ*, 4:52–53.

12. August Strindberg, *Storm Weather*, in *The Chamber Plays*, translated by Seabury Quinn, Jr. and Kenneth Petersen (New York: E. P. Dutton, 1962), p. 46.

13. Goethe, *Götz von Berlichingen*, act 3, scene 18. *The Complete Works of Johann Wolfgang von Goethe*, vol. 6 (New York: P. F. Collier & Son, n.d.), pp. 258–59. The translation is by Sir Walter Scott.

Chapter Six

1. V. S. Pritchett, "Hearing from Chekhov," *The New York Review of Books*, June 28, 1973, p. 4.

2. *MOZ*, 7:111.

3. Anton Chekhov, quoted in Pritchett, p. 3.

4. Charles Baudelaire, *The Painter of Modern Life and*

Other Essays, translated and edited by Jonathan Maine (London: Phaidon Press, 1964), p. 204.

5. Frederic Jameson, *Marxism and Form* (Princeton, N.J.: Princeton University Press, 1971), p. 42.

6. *Ibid.*, p. 38.

Selected Bibliography

PRIMARY SOURCES

1. In Japanese

There has been a number of sets of collected works of Ōgai, and the two newest are the best.

The eight volume *Mori Ōgai zenshū* (Tokyo: Chikuma shobo, 1971) includes all Ōgai's prose writings, plus a good selection of his poetry, drama, and essays. Despite the title, however, it is not complete. This edition is especially useful in that the editors have provided copious notes on all texts, and their comments and elucidations are generally helpful and straightforward.

The thirty-eight volume *Ōgai zenshū* (Tokyo: Iwanami shoten, 1972) is still, at this writing, in the process of being issued. When completed, it will include all of Ōgai's poetry, translations, articles, letters, etc. The texts are beautifully printed, but no notes of any kind are provided.

There is an endless number of collections of Ōgai stories in a wide variety of formats, but in general the complete sets provide more accurate texts and better commentaries.

2. Translations

A certain amount of Ōgai's work has appeared in translation, although the quality, especially in the earlier translations, is regrettably variable. There is a complete listing of available translations in *Modern Japanese Literature in Western Translations, a Bibliography* (Tokyo: International House of Japan Library, 1972), which contains the most up-to-date information available.

Following are the most important translations now available.

MN is the journal *Monumenta Nipponica*, published by Sophia University in Tokyo.

BOWRING, RICHARD. "Utakata no ki." *MN* 29 (1974), 247–251.

BRAZELL, KAREN "The Courier" ("Fumizukai"). *MN* 26 (1971), 100–14.

DILWORTH, DAVID and THOMAS RIMER. "Kanzan Jittoku." *MN* 26 (1971), 159–67.

DILWORTH, DAVID. "Suginohara Shina." *MN* 26 (1971), 169–79.

DOWER, JOHN W. "Cups" ("Sakazuki"). *MN* 26 (1971), 139–42.

————. "Delusion" ("Mōsō"). *MN* 25 (1970), 415–30.

————. 'Exoricism" ("Tsuina"). *MN* 26 (1971), 133–38.

————. "Snake" ("Hebi"). *MN* 26 (1971), 121–32.

FUKUDA, TSUTOMU. "Sansho Dayū." Tokyo: Hokuseido Press, 1970.

MORRIS, IVAN. "Under Reconstruction" ("Fushinchū"). In *Modern Japanese Stories,* edited by Ivan Morris. Tokyo and Rutland, Vermont: Charles E. Tuttle Co., 1962, pp. 35–44.

MURRAY, DARCY. "Half a Day" ("Hannichi"). *MN* 28 (1973), 347–61.

NINOMIYA KAZUJI and SANFORD GOLDSTEIN. *Vita Sexualis.* Tokyo and Rutland, Vermont: Charles E. Tuttle Co., 1972.

OCHIAI KINGO and SANFORD GOLDSTEIN. *Wild Geese* (Gan). Tokyo and Rutland, Vermont: Charles E. Tuttle Co., 1959. This translation is also available in the collection *The World of Japanese Fiction,* edited by Arthur Lewis and Yoshinobu Hakutani. New York: E. P. Dutton, 1973, pp. 89–179.

SINCLAIR, G. M. and SUITA KAZO. "As If" ("Ka no yō ni"). In *Tokyo People: Three Stories from the Japanese.* Tokyo: Keibunkan, 1925, pp. 61–117.

SKRZYPCZAK, EDMUND R. "Takasebune." *MN* 26 (1971), 181–89.

TAKEMOTO TORAO. "Hanako." In *Paulownia: Seven Stories from Contemporary Japanese Writers.* N.Y.: Duffield, 1918, pp. 35–51.

————. "Pier." In *Paulownia,* pp. 56–68.

WILSON, WILLIAM RITCHIE. "The Last Will and Testament of Okitsu Yagoemon." *MN* 26 (1971), 143–58.

ZOLBROD, LEON. "The Girl Who Danced" ("Maihime"). In *The*

Language of Love, edited by Michael R. Martin. New York: Bantam Books, 1964, pp. 1–14.

David Dilworth and the present writer have translated and edited under the auspices of UNESCO a volume of translations of Ōgai's historical writing. Most of the *Monumenta Nipponica* translations listed above will be reprinted in the volume, as well as new translations of "Abe Ichizoku," "Gojingahara no katakiuchi," "Gyogenki," "Jiisan baasan," "Kuriyama Daizen," "Sahashi Jingorō," "Saigo no ikku," "Saiki Koi," "Sakai jiken," "Sanshō dayū," "Tokō Tahei," "Tsuge Shirōzaemon," and "Yasui Fujin." The book is scheduled to appear in 1975.

SECONDARY SOURCES

1. In Japanese

The amount of secondary material on Ōgai in Japanese is enormous. The items listed below were of particular interest to me in preparing this basic outline of Ōgai's life and work, and those readers who know Japanese and wish to examine the critical texts on Ōgai will find all of them of interest.

HASEGAWA IZUMI. *Mori Ōgai*. Tokyo: Meiji shoin, 1970. A brief biography of Ōgai that includes a number of unusual photographs, maps, and other pictorial information of superior quality.

INAGAKI TATSURŌ. *Mori Ōgai hikkei*. Tokyo: Gakutōsha, 1968. An invaluable guide to Ōgai: chronologies, descriptions of each work, essays on various literary and philosophical aspects of his writings. A fine handbook.

OKAZAKI YOSHIE. *Ōgai to teinen*. Tokyo: Hōbunkan, 1969. A provocative and authoritative biography, tracing the ideas of "resignation" (*teinen*) as they developed in Ōgai's mind throughout his career.

SATO HARUO. "Jinchū no tategoto." In *Sato Haruo zenshū*, vol. 10. (Tokyo: Kōdansha, 1967). The finest essay written on Ōgai's poetry, which concentrates on the "Uta Nikki." Sato was a fine poet himself, and his comments are both precise and perceptive.

SHIBUKAWA GYŌ. *Mori Ōgai, sakka to sakuhin.* Tokyo: Chikuma shobo, 1964. An unpretentious book that contains much of the necessary basic information on Ōgai and the development of his ideas from a literary point of view.

YAMAZAKI MASAKAZU. *Ōgai tatakau kachō.* Tokyo: Kawade shobo, 1973. An unusual and personal analysis of Ōgai's personality and the relation between aspects of his personal life and his literature. Yamazaki, a fine modern playwright, has great literary insight.

2. In English

BRAZELL, KAREN. "Mori Ōgai in Germany." *MN* 26 (1971), 77–100. A fine introductory treatment of the subject.

DOWER, JOHN W. "Mori Ōgai: Eminent Bystander." In *Papers on Japan*, vol. 2, Harvard East Asian Research Center, August, 1963. A lengthy discussion of Ōgai's aesthetic borrowings from German writers and his own sense of "resignation." Rather technical, but a number of stimulating insights.

HASEGAWA, IZUMI. "Mori Ōgai," *Japan Quarterly* 12 (April, 1965), 237–44. A brief but very well constructed biography of Ōgai, easily the best concise account available in English.

JOHNSON, ERIC W. "The Historical Fiction and Biography of Mori Ōgai." *The Journal of the Association of Teachers of Japanese* 8 (Nov., 1972), 7–25. Originally a lecture presented for the Association of Asian Studies.

KATŌ SHŪICHI. "Japanese Writers and Modernization." In *Changing Japanese Attitudes toward Modernization*, edited by Marius Jansen. (Princeton, N.J.: Princeton University Press, 1965). A fine treatment of Ōgai in the context of modernizing Japan.

KOSAKA MASAAKI, ed. *Japanese Thought in the Meiji Period.* Tokyo: Toyo Bunko, 1958. The section "Natsume Sōseki, Mori Ōgai and Naturalism" has an extended discussion of Ōgai's fundamental ideas.

MIYOSHI MASAO. *Accomplices of Silence: The Modern Japanese Novel.* Berkeley and Los Angeles: The University of

California Press, 1974. The chapter on Ōgai, while rather severe, contains a number of subtle and accomplished observations; all in all, one of the most stimulating pieces available.

MORITA, JAMES R. "Shigarami-zōshi." *MN* 24 (1969), 51–58. An account of Ōgai's first literary magazine.

MOTOFUJI, FRANK. "Mori Ōgai: Three Plays and the Problem of Identity," *Modern Drama* 9 (Feb., 1967), 412–30. The only account in English concerning Ōgai's work in the theater. Good summaries of the three plays discussed.

OKAZAKI YOSHIE. *Japanese Literature in the Meiji Era.* Tokyo: Toyo Bunko, 1955. Scattered throughout the volume are a number of stimulating discussions of Ōgai's work.

ORIGAS, JEAN JACQUES. "Sur le style de Mori Ōgai," *Transactions of the International Conference of Orientalists* 9 (1964), 15–34. A discussion of changes in Ōgai's language as Japanese modernized.

SWANN, THOMAS E. "The Problem of 'Utakata no Ki.'" *MN* 29 (1974), 264–281. A fine analysis of the story and its background.

Index

(The works of Mori Ōgai are listed under his name)